THE JOURNEY

Learning to Walk in the Way

DR. WILLIE JOUBERT

The Journey

tellwell

Tellwell Talent
www.tellwell.ca

ISBN
978-0-2288-5920-8 (Hardcover)
978-0-2288-5919-2 (Paperback)
978-0-2288-5921-5 (eBook)

TABLE OF CONTENTS

ACKNOWLEDGEMENTS

I want to express my sincere appreciation to my wife, Eda, who yet again dared to walk with me as we continued the journey into the wilderness. Only you will know the price that was paid and I thank you for walking the extra miles with me.

I want to thank Peter Saffery for his encouragement and help. You have stepped into our lives at a critical time to be a blessing. Thank you from the bottom of our hearts.

I also thank the Lord for others that walked with us or joined with us at crucial times in the journey. I was tempted to put names down, but the list is long and I do not want to run the risk of missing a key name. Further, there are many that carried us in the journey as the Spirit worked in the body of our Lord without us having been aware of it. Ultimately it is about the Lord and to him be the glory and praise.

DEDICATION

This book is dedicated to the no names that are willing to let go of everything to serve the Lord as they follow the Spirit. May God bless you in your ministry and take you on incredible journeys into the wilderness to release the water of life so that the desert may bloom.

INTRODUCTION

As I reflected on our personal journey of faith, we sought to pursue the Lord willing to go wherever the Spirit may lead us. In time we found ourselves outside of what most people (including evangelical friends) would consider to be "the church." In many ways the journey forced us to rethink most of what we had learned (and taught!) about the church. In fact, as I talked to a friend about this one day, he used the term "the world of the church" and this really put the picture in perspective for me. I want to challenge you to consider this with me for a moment.

The church as I know it from experience as member and former pastor operates much like any worldly business or organization. Leaders who are elected or appointed run it. They oversee and manage the programs and handle the budget, very much like the local businesses in town. There are set hours of operation and policies to guide the operation, etc. In fact, as I spoke with another good friend re finances in the church, he stated that the church is a business and needed to be run as a business.

He is right in that the church in North America is certainly nothing else than a business, often poorly run, but operating like any worldly business. Most of the time the products and services we offer are of a spiritual nature or packaged in a spiritual container. These are advertised in the local media e. g. the services, sermon titles and special programs run by the local churches competing for their share of the marketplace. **However, this is not the church that we find in the pages of the New Testament! Moreover, we are in the world, but not to be of this world, as we see in the prayer of our Lord just before he was arrested:** *"I will remain in the world no longer, but they are still in the world, and I am coming to you. Holy Father, protect them by the power of your name – the name you gave me – so that they may be one as we are one. My prayer is not that you take them out of this world, but that you protect them from the evil one. They are not of the world, even as I am not of it. Sanctify them by the truth; your word is truth. As you sent me into the world, I have sent them into the world."* John 17:11 and 15-18

As we pursued Jesus, we were led to the Scriptures again and again. God set up divine appointments and one of these brought me to the letter to the Hebrews, which came to life in a miraculous way[1]. This confirmed the revelation I had about the church structure and leadership models in a very simple way: Most of what we consider to be "church" in the North American mindset is nothing else than a "Christianized version

[1] For details see my book "Ordinary people extraordinary royal priests."

of the Old Testament Levitical system." Thus, church is a business run by a Levitical caste of clergy and lay leaders overseeing programs and maintaining buildings for these programs. **However, Jesus Christ is the High Priest in the order of Melchizedek and in him this old system was totally abolished! Our God does not live in buildings built by human hands with mortar and stone and maintained by a separate class of people! In Christ all of us have become royal priests and the division of his body, the church, into laity and clergy (by whatever name) is sin!**

Having understood this, we knew there was no way back and no way to compromise. We were already outside and found that it was a wilderness - and yet in this wilderness we came to live with the Lord in a powerful and living way. Many of the things we formerly believed and practiced were abandoned and we paid the price of rejection by many. Having been involved with major prayer initiatives on different levels, we found that the Spirit led us to spend time with him in the wilderness and took us away from the 'major initiatives.' In this process Hebrews 13:11-12 spoke very loud to us: *The high priest carries the blood of animals into the Most Holy Place as a sin offering, but the bodies are burned outside the camp. And so Jesus suffered outside the city gate to make the people holy through his own blood. Let us then go to him outside the camp, bearing the disgrace he bore. For here we do not have an enduring city, but we are looking for a city that is to come.* These verses spoke to us even more as we had moved in circles where there was a growing tendency to see 'pastors and intercessors' as spiritual gatekeepers for the cities! Like Jesus who walked through the gate (symbolic of the Levitical control and judgment by the Levitical leadership) and suffered outside, we passed through the gate into the wilderness. **Our very presence and message ran into the face of the leadership structure of the church as we knew it and we soon realized we were outside and judged by many with whom we formerly walked. But once outside we also found many others who had journeyed through the gate to tabernacle (camp) with God in the wilderness and began to walk in "The Way."**

The Lord then opened our eyes to see in a new way. We began to see so many as Jesus did. For the first time we began to understand the Scripture that said Jesus had compassion on the people, for they were like sheep without a shepherd - even many in "the church!" We began to rejoice with others as we simply met in homes and wherever we could and instead of "going to church and doing the programs," we learned how to be the church. It is a process! It does not come easy, for there is a lot of baggage that needs to be shed as we move from the comfort of the four walls and the oversight and control of the Levitical priests to tabernacle in the wilderness and live in the freedom of the Spirit. As the Spirit leads, I will share more about this journey and the lessons we learned, so that others who are considering this journey may have some guideposts. **However, one thing I do need to say is this: It is more**

than worth it! We have decided to follow Jesus - outside the gates of Levitical structures - and there is no turning back!

The first step is always the most important. Without that the journey will never become a reality. The first step begins with a decision to bow the knee before Jesus and to be willing to follow whatever the cost in obedience to his voice. Let us look at this as if for the first time and listen to the Spirit.

A RADICAL STEP OF FAITH

Just before Christmas 1967 I found myself at a summer job in Vereeniging, South Africa as student. It was at the end of my second year as student in Chemical Engineering and I was working for the Rand Water Board as part of the scholarship agreement that would lead to a full-time job with the company, once I completed my studies. During this time, I was seeking the Lord and sensed that my life would radically change. On a Sunday night I was listening to a message on the radio referring to 2 Timothy 4:10 and challenging "a Demas in the world to walk into his call to full time ministry." The Spirit clearly showed me that I was that Demas who had been resisting the call of God and I bowed the knee and accepted the call. As I understood it at the time, it could only mean to become a pastor in the church. I was born and raised in the Dutch Reformed Church and the pathway was set in stone. It meant completing a degree with at least 2 years of Hebrew and Greek and one year of Latin, to gain entrance to the Seminary for three more years of study followed by another year of preparation to enter the ministry.

As I considered the options I decided that it made sense to first complete the Engineering degree and the commitment of four years working for the Rand Water Board as per the scholarship agreement, rather than find another way to repay the two years tuition and support money and begin with the ministry courses. I reasoned that I could complete the language requirements through correspondence, while I worked full time in a good job and walk away with no debt and money saved to cover the cost at Seminary. **It made good sense; except I did not check with the Spirit if this was the way to follow!**

As I resumed my studies in January, I was set to complete my third year in Engineering. However, my interest was no longer in this and soon I fell behind in my studies. Within a couple of months, I faced the fact that I needed to make a decision to work like never before (without which I would fail and pay a huge price) or I had to change course! I spent time in prayer and then asked the Lord to give me a clear answer – and simply flipped the Bible open. I knew this was not the prescribed way to find answers, but I was desperate and God did answer! The Bible opened and I read Matthew 8:18-22:

When Jesus saw the crowd around him, he gave orders to cross to the other side of the lake. Then a teacher of the law came to him and said, "Teacher, I will follow you wherever you go."

Jesus replied: "Foxes have holes and the birds of the air have nests, but the Son of man has no place to lay his head."

Another disciple came to him and said: "Lord, first let me go and bury my father."

But Jesus told him: "Follow me and let the dead bury their own dead."

I knew I had to submit and at that moment my studies in Engineering were over. God opened the door that I was allowed to change courses (even though it was past the deadline set by the University). Afterwards I found a job and a place to stay and the opportunity to study after hours. Three years later I graduated as Bachelor of Arts majoring in Greek and Hebrew. This in turn opened other doors, as I was able to do post graduate studies in Semitic languages while at Seminary. Those studies opened another door as lecturer in Semitics that allowed me to complete a Ph. D. in Old Testament studies years later. In time another door opened when I was accepted into the Presbyterian Church in Canada and we immigrated as family.

Years later this same lesson became very real in a different way as I walked out of the Institutional Church in obedience to the call of Christ. However, I thank God for what I had learned so many years before and it is time to look at the key issue: **Jesus calls us to**

walk in radical authenticity and obedience.[2] **To follow him is to lay aside our own agendas and ideas and to be willing to submit in obedience whatever the cost. He set the example when he died on the cross and he calls us to take up our cross and follow him. In a word – we are to be radically obedient to his voice. This is very clearly outlined by Paul in Romans 12:1-2:**

Therefore, I urge you, brothers, in view of God's mercy, to offer your bodies as living sacrifices, holy and pleasing to God – this is your spiritual act of worship. Do not conform any longer to the pattern of this world, but be transformed through the renewal of your mind. Then you will be able to test and approve what God's will is – his good, pleasing and perfect will.

The first transformation that needs to take place in my mind is to be willing to submit in obedience to the voice of Jesus and to follow the guidance of the Spirit. **This is a process and does not happen overnight. However, the process only happens as we submit to what the Spirit is saying at the time and then take the step of faith that leads to the next revelation. Thus, if I hear the voice of the Lord and the Spirit reveals truth, I need to respond in faith and obedience at that time to be in position for the next step of the journey. This is exactly the point many stop in their walk, as they are not willing to move in faith.**

[2] For more details see my book "Radical Authenticity – Being the church in the world 3."

For everyone there are crucial Kairos (Greek term meaning divinely set times) moments in their faith where they are stretched to walk in a new revelation and many get stuck for long times (and sometimes permanently), because they are not willing to move out of the comfort zone.

The question to each of us is this: Am I willing to allow the Spirit to apply the word of God to my life in order to cut through the veil separating my soul (will, mind and emotions) from my spirit as Hebrews 4:12 says, so that the Spirit can transform my mindset? Only then will I walk in the Spirit and not in the flesh! Only then will I find that God's will is indeed good, pleasing and perfect. This is not a theoretical question and many will respond that they are indeed open to hear the Spirit and act in obedience to the word. I question this, as the reality I have observed is very different. Let us take the issue of church leadership for example. Most evangelical churches accept and follow a Levitical system and in practice deny the priesthood of the believer. The division between clergy and laity is not to be found in the New Testament, yet is practiced and upheld by virtually every denomination (including those who prefer to be called non-denominational). This is one of the most crucial transformations needed in the mind in response to the truth of the word of God. However, when weighing the cost, most in leadership and many in the pews are not willing to pay the price – and having been there myself, I understand this. It means that the current paid position of pastor has to be abandoned and those called to leadership are to become servants – working in the world or living by faith. To walk away from this Levitical system and practice the New Testament order of Melchizedek comes with a steep price for those accustomed to the salaries and allowances and tax perks offered by the religious system. Therefore, most in leadership will not allow the sword of the Word to cut through the veil between spirit and soul and make the choice by the Spirit, but choose to operate by using the Old Testament Levitical model and worldly reason to construct and maintain the status quo and with that their position of privilege and power. The other side of the coin is that many in the pew are willing to submit to this model and to support it, for it is no different from the corporate world they know where leaders rule and oversee the operation. They are not willing to question the system and would rather pay "a pastor" to represent them before God than spend time in the Word and learn to hear God's voice and walk in the Spirit. It is no different than the picture that Jeremiah observed when he wrote the prophetic words recorded in Jeremiah 5:30-31: *A horrible and shocking thing has happened in the land: The prophets prophesy lies, the priests rule by their own authority and my people love it this way. But what will you do in the end?*

This is serious! We have done exactly what Israel did when they rejected the Lord's rule and sought a king like the other nations.[3] We have rejected the order of Melchizedek and instituted our "Christianized" versions of the Levitical priesthood with priests ruling as kings over the people, even though Jesus expressly said it ought not be so when he was approached by the mother of John and James about the matter as we read in Matthew 20:25-28: *Jesus called them together and said: "You know that the rulers of the Gentiles lord it over them and their high officials exercise authority over them. Not so with you! Instead, whoever wants to be great among you must be your servant, and whoever wants to be first must be your slave – just as the Son of man did not come to be served, but to serve and to give his life as a ransom for many."*

To cover our disobedience, we have spiritualized this matter of our "kings" by giving them religious titles – pope, pastor, the reverend, minister, bishop, etc. We help them build their little kingdoms (churches and ministries) and submit to their authority and serve them – and further spiritualize the ungodly submission to men and women by calling them "servant leaders." God's people are again destroyed because of a lack of knowledge, as the vast majority in the church (including those in the "evangelical and Spirit filled" churches) do not know that they are indeed called and appointed to be royal priests in the order of Melchizedek and they do not need the world of the church with its buildings,

[3] As we started on this journey God opened our eyes to these realities and led us to study the Scriptures. As a result, I wrote the book "Restoring the broken foundations," which deals with these matters in more details.

priests, programs and bureaucracy, but they need to be the church in the world. Many who are in leadership in the church know this, but are unwilling to address the issue, for it gets too close to home! The price is too high and so they find a spiritual reason to avoid addressing this, just as king Ahaz did when Isaiah approached him as recorded in Isaiah 7. Let us look at this story and the lesson for us.

The background to the story is as follows: The kingdoms of Judah and Israel as well as the neighboring kingdom of Aram began feeling the pressure of the growing super power of Assyria. Judah was a little further removed and less important from a strategic point of view, but was being pressured by the other two kings to join a coalition to stop the Assyrian expansion. The word of the Lord was to ignore the pressure and simply wait it out, rather than being drawn into the regional politics and wars. If Ahaz did not heed this, the escalating crisis would bring the Assyrian army to Judah with great devastation. Isaiah known as reputable prophet together with his son, Shear Jashub (a prophetic name meaning "a remnant shall return,") went to meet the king as he was checking the water supply into the city in case of a siege. Isaiah delivered the message and then realized that the king would not heed the word of the Lord. With that the prophet challenged the king to test the prophetic word by seeking a sign from the Lord. Then we read the following in Isaiah 7:12-17:

But Ahaz said, "I will not ask; I will not put the Lord to the test."

Then Isaiah said, "Hear now, you house of David! Is it not enough to try the patience of men? Will you try the patience of my God also? Therefore, the Lord himself will give you a sign: The young lady[4] *will be with child and will give birth to a son and will call him Emmanuel. He will eat curds and honey when he knows enough to reject the wrong and choose the right. But before the boy knows enough to reject the wrong and choose the right, the land of the two kings you dread will be laid waste. The Lord will bring on you and on your people and on the house of your father a time unlike any since Ephraim broke away from Judah – he will bring the king of Assyria."*

Following this Isaiah expanded the prophetic word with more detail re the devastation to follow and also the prophetic promise of the returning remnant tied to his son's name. However, let us get to the heart of the issue for us. **Many in the church, especially leaders, when confronted with the truth about the fact that they follow a Levitical order instead of the New Testament order of Melchizedek, respond like Ahaz, unwilling to heed the word of God. They seek reasons why they can ignore the truth by trying to sound spiritual and cover the disobedience. Most counter that God has used the Levitical church for a long time and thus will continue to do so. However, in the**

[4] The Hebrew word means "a young lady" and as such could imply "virgin." In this context it is the former, but in the Greek translation of the Old Testament it was translated as "virgin." Matthew used the Greek translation in a very different context to apply this to the birth of Jesus in Matthew 1:23.

same way God used the kingship in the Old Testament, upon which we have built the current leadership structure of the ruling elite in the church to a large degree. God actually blessed it at times, even though it began in rebellion to his Kingship (read 1 Samuel 8, especially verse 7) and would not last. The Old Testament kingship came to an end, but God's kingdom that Israel had rejected in favor of an earthly king was restored in Christ. Like the kingship in the Old Testament, the leadership model followed in the church for 1700 years has been a mixed bag bringing blessing and curses upon the God's people. It is time to go to the foundations and restore the broken foundations as the Word of God clearly teaches. The false humility used to avoid the truth and to walk it out will bring only further destruction to the people of God as it did in the days of Ahaz.

Let those who have an ear to hear, hear what the Spirit is saying and let us walk out of the world of the church and into the freedom of the Spirit. Let us follow Jesus past the gate of control and judgment and outside the walls and the camp and let us walk into the wilderness where there is freedom (Hebrews 13:11-14). Let us let go of the baggage of ecclesiastical worldly traditions and the rule of men, however well intentioned, or anointed, and allow the Lord to

speak to us as we tabernacle with him. In the process every one of us will hear the voice of God and his word will cut through the veil, so that his Spirit in us will transform our minds to become more like him and our lives will show the fruit that will reveal his Kingdom to the world.

As we observed above, there are many that get the revelation, but refuse to put it into practice. This is not written for them. Others are like the Israelites that passed through the Red Sea, but when the reality of the journey through the wilderness set in, they wanted to go back and rebelled. Thus, they move out of the Institutional Church, but seek to restore the old system and eventually end up where they came from. This is also not for them. **This book is written for those who truly desire to follow the Spirit in radical obedience, wherever he may lead them. It is for those who, like Abraham, will journey to the Promised Land and not turn back.** I simply want to share some areas where we had to radically adjust our mindsets in order to walk in the freedom of the Spirit. These are not in any order of importance, but simply words of encouragement as I look back to our journey to date. Thus, put on your walking shoes and let us walk together, keeping our eyes on Jesus, the author and finisher of our faith.

ADJUSTING TO FREEDOM

I believe the most difficult thing for most that walk out of the Institutional Church is to adjust to the freedom of the Spirit. In fact, the reason that many return to the slavery of the Institutional Church is because they are not able to handle the freedom offered in Christ. It calls for a radical change in mindset and a new paradigm of living. In a very real way, it is not much different than the adjustment the early Jewish believers had to make, especially when the gospel reached the Gentiles. This first outreach to the Gentiles came through the divine vision to Peter recorded in Acts 10. The Lord had to prepare him by giving him the same vision three times. In this vision he saw something like a large sheet filled with all kinds of unclean animals being let down to earth by its four corners. Each time a voice called him to get up, kill and eat and Peter responded by saying he could not as he had never eaten anything impure or unclean. Each time the voice would speak again, saying: "Do not call anything impure that God has made clean!" This vision preceded the arrival of the servants sent by Cornelius as instructed by the Lord and when they arrived, the Spirit told Peter about them and he was sent by the Spirit to the Gentile house to share the message of Jesus. The door to the Gentiles was opened wide as the Spirit filled them in the same way as he did with the Jewish believers on the day of Pentecost. Upon his return to Jerusalem Peter was criticized by many about his visit to the Gentile home, but when he shared the details, they had no objections and praised the Lord for the new life granted to even the Gentiles.

However, this issue continued to be a thorny one and in time as the message spread among the Gentiles, some from Jewish background continued to insist that these new believers had to be circumcised as we read in Acts 15:1. This led to a special meeting with the apostles and elders in Jerusalem which again confirmed that Gentile believers did not have to become Jewish and follow Jewish customs (Acts 15:1-35). Even so, in time some would again pressure the Gentiles to follow Jewish customs, particularly the circumcision and even Peter of all people did this, until Paul rebuked him openly about his hypocrisy (Galatians 2:11-21). In fact, the letter to the Galatians is a very good example to illustrate how people often struggle to adjust to freedom and how religious spirits can enslave free people through religious traditions. At the same time this letter illustrates how former slaves struggle to handle freedom and how they often fall back into bondage. Let us look at this in the light of this letter written by Paul.

In Galatians 1:6-7 Paul outlined the issue in clear terms when he says: *I am astonished that you are so quickly deserting the one who called you by the grace of Christ and are turning to a different gospel which is really no gospel at all. Evidently some people are throwing you into confusion and are trying to pervert the gospel of Christ.* Later in Galatians 3:1-3 he wrote: *You foolish Galatians! Who has bewitched you? Before your very eyes Christ was clearly portrayed as crucified. I would like to learn just one thing from you: Did you receive the Spirit by observing the law or by believing what you heard? Are you so foolish? After beginning with the Spirit, are you now trying to attain your goal by human effort?* **This is really the issue: It is the choice between human effort and walking in the Spirit by faith. It is the choice between pleasing men or pleasing God as Paul wrote in Galatians 1:10.** The Galatians started in the Spirit, but were later convinced by the Judaizers that they also had to become religious observers of the Judaic traditions and submit to the Old Testament laws as interpreted and practiced by the religious Jews, especially the rite of circumcision. They exchanged the freedom offered in Christ for religious legalism. In doing this they turned their backs on the heart of the message of Jesus who was clearly portrayed as crucified and *redeemed us from the curse of the law by becoming a curse for us, for it is written: "Cursed is everyone who is hung on a tree."* (Galatians 3:13)

As a former Pharisee Paul understood the issue very well. However, his life was changed in the dust of the Damascus road when he met the crucified Jesus as risen Lord. In his own words recorded in Philippians 3:7-15:

But whatever was to my profit I now consider loss for the sake of Christ. What is more, I consider everything a loss compared to the surpassing greatness of knowing Christ Jesus my Lord, for whose sake I have lost all things. I consider them rubbish, that I might gain Christ and be found in him, not having a righteousness of my own that comes from the law, but that which is through faith in Christ – the righteousness that comes from God and is by faith. I want to know Christ and the power of his resurrection and the fellowship of his sufferings, becoming like him in his death, and so, somehow, to attain to the resurrection from the dead. Not that I have already obtained all this, or have already been made perfect, but I press on to take a hold of that for which Christ took a hold of me. Brothers, I do not consider myself yet to have taken a hold of it. But one thing I do: Forgetting what is behind and straining toward what is ahead, I press on toward the goal to win the prize for which God has called me heavenward in Christ Jesus. All of us who are mature should take such a view of things."

In Christ and in knowing him we find everything we ever need. In him we find the righteousness that religious legalism can never give and the freedom to walk in the Spirit through faith and in relationship with Jesus. In the words of Paul in Colossians 2:6-15: *So then, just as you received Christ Jesus as Lord, continue to live in him, rooted and built up in him, strengthened in the faith as you were taught, and overflowing with thankfulness. See to it that no one takes you captive through hollow and deceptive philosophy, which depends on human tradition and the basic principles of this world rather than on Christ. For in Christ all the fullness of the Deity lives in bodily form, and you have been given fullness in Christ, who is the head over every* *power and authority. In him you were also circumcised, in the putting off of the sinful nature, not with a circumcision done by the hands of men but with the circumcision done by Christ, having been buried with him in baptism and raised with him through your faith in the power of God, who raised him from the dead. When you were dead in your sins and in the uncircumcision of your sinful nature, God made you alive with Christ. He forgave us all our sins, having canceled the written code, with its regulations, that was against us and stood opposed to us; he took it away nailing it to the cross. And having disarmed the powers and authorities he made a public spectacle of them, triumphing over them by the cross.*

Being in Christ sets us free from religious traditions and regulations. Being in Christ opens the door to a relationship with the Father and the security it gives. This is beautifully described in Galatians 3:23-4:7: *Before this faith came, we were held prisoners by the law, locked up until faith should be revealed. So the law was put in charge to lead us to Christ that we might be justified by faith. Now that faith has come, we are no longer under the supervision of the law. You are all sons of God through faith in Jesus Christ. There is neither Jew nor Greek, slave nor free, male nor female, for you are all one in Christ Jesus. If you belong to Christ then you are Abraham's seed, and heirs according to the promise. What I am saying is that as long as the heir is a child, he is no different from a slave, although he owns the whole estate. He is subject to guardians and trustees until the time set by the father. So also, when we were children we were in slavery under the principles of the world. But when the time had fully come, God sent his son, born of a woman, born under law, to redeem those under law, so that we might receive the full rights of sons. Because you are sons, God sent the Spirit of his*

Son into our hearts, the Spirit who calls out, 'Abba, Father.' So you are no longer a slave, but a son, and since you are a son, God has also made you an heir.

Let us look at this again and see how simple it really is. We will walk in freedom led by the Spirit as sons of God in Christ or we will be in bondage as slaves to human rules and regulations. We will find our security in our position as sons of the Father or we will seek security in our performance of the rules and regulations set up by religious legalists and being judged by humans. We will be led by the Spirit of Christ or driven by the spirit of religious legalism. Each of us will hear the voice of God and follow him or choose to have someone else discern 'the voice of the Lord' and set up rules and traditions for us to follow in order to belong to 'the church.' The sad part is that many in the church are in bondage and have been taken captive through hollow and deceptive philosophy which depends on human tradition and the principles of this world rather than on Christ. Many refuse to see this and will vehemently argue that they are not (and maybe as you read this you will want to immediately respond that it is not true or at least does not apply to you personally), but bear with me for a moment and read with me how Paul continued the passage above in Galatians 4:8-11 and **let the Spirit speak through these words**: *Formerly, when you did not know God, you were slaves to those who by nature are not gods. But now that you know God – or rather are known by God – how is it that you are turning back to those weak and miserable principles? Do you wish to be enslaved by them all over again?*

You are observing special days and months and seasons and years! I fear for you, that somehow, I have wasted my efforts on you.

Without going into detail, most of the Institutional Church today observes special days and seasons. In fact, most believers in the western world follow a written or unwritten law that Sunday be a special day set aside for specific times of worship, often tied to the Old Testament Sabbath. Depending on the local church's background and affiliation, specific rules and expectations are tied to the observance of Sundays. In addition, many follow the 'Church Year' with special observances of Advent, Christmas, Lent and Easter. Further there are the traditional celebrations of Thanksgiving, Mother's Day and Sunday School's Rally Day and Award Sunday, etc. There are also many other rules and expectations in various churches, e. g. tithing and giving to support the local church and its programs, membership tied to the local body, dietary rules, especially about the use of alcoholic beverages (including whether or not wine or grape juice is served at communion), the handling of the sacraments (or emblems) and particularly who is to handle these, qualifications for office holders in the church, often tied to specific academic requirements linked to specific 'approved' institutions. With that in mind let us read Colossians 2:16-23: *Therefore, do not let anyone judge you by what you eat or drink, or with regard to a religious festival, a New Moon celebration or a Sabbath Day. These are a shadow of the things that were to come; the reality however is found in Christ. Do not let anyone who delights in false humility and the worship of angels disqualify you for the prize. Such a person goes into great detail about what he has seen, and his unspiritual mind puffs him up with idle notions. He has lost connection with the head, from whom the whole body, supported and held together by its ligaments and sinews, grows as God causes it to grow. Since you have died with Christ to the basic principles of the world, why, as though you still belonged to it, do you submit to its rules: 'Do not handle! Do not taste! Do not touch!' These are destined to perish with use, because they are based on human commands and teachings. Such teachings indeed have an appearance of wisdom, with their self-imposed worship, their false humility and their harsh treatment of the body, but they lack any value in restraining sensual indulgence.*

The truth is that much of what we do in our churches is nothing else but following rules and regulations to control lives. These things do have an appearance of wisdom, but like the legalism of the pharisaic traditions, simply put people in bondage and slavery. The law cannot set people free. The reality is found in Christ and in him alone! In him we received the Spirit of sonship by whom we cry, "Abba, Father!" In him we have access to the Father and can boldly enter into his presence. In Christ we have received a new covenant in his blood, as we read in Hebrews 8:6-13: *But the ministry Jesus has received is superior to theirs as the covenant of which he is mediator is superior to the old one and is founded on better promises. For if there had been nothing wrong with that first covenant, no place would have been sought for another. But God found fault with the people and said:*

"The time is coming, declares the Lord,
when I will make a new covenant
with the house of Israel
and with the house of Judah.
It will not be like the covenant
I made with their forefathers
when I took them out by the hand
to lead them out of Egypt,
Because they did not remain faithful to my covenant,
and I turned away from them, declares the Lord.
This is the covenant I will make with the house of Israel
after that time, declares the Lord.
I will put my laws in their minds
and write them on their hearts.
I will be their God
and they will be my people.
No longer will a man teach his neighbor,
or a man his brother saying, 'Know the Lord,'
for they will all know me,
from the least of them to the greatest.
For I will forgive their wickedness
and will remember their sins no more."
By calling this covenant 'new,' he has made the first one obsolete
and what is obsolete and aging will soon disappear.

Instead of legalistic rules and regulations as in the old covenant, **we have received a new covenant with the Spirit of Christ guiding each individual member of the body of the Lord.** In the words of Jesus in John 10:4 *his sheep know his voice and follow him.* In 1 John 2:26-27 we read: *I am writing these things to you about* *those who are trying to lead you astray. As for you, the anointing you received from him remains in you, and you do not need anyone to teach you. But as his anointing teaches you about all things and as that anointing is real, not counterfeit – just as it has taught you, remain in him.* Thus, we do not need any person teaching us what to do and laying down rules and regulations for church membership and conduct. We have been set free from this by Jesus, the Son, and *whom the Son has set free, is free indeed* (John 8:36). In fact, in 2 Corinthians 3 Paul also compared the ministry of the old covenant through Moses with the ministry of Jesus and says in 2 Corinthians 3:15-18: *Even to this day when Moses is read, a veil covers their hearts. But whenever anyone turns to the Lord, the veil is taken away. Now the Lord is Spirit, and wherever the Spirit of the Lord is, there is freedom. And we, who with unveiled faces all reflect the Lord's glory, are being transformed into his likeness with ever-increasing glory, which comes from the Lord, who is the Spirit.*

Let us begin to connect these dots to complete the picture. **The church was never intended to be an organization. It is the body of Christ with the risen Lord as head. It is a living entity and is spiritual in nature. It cannot be "incorporated" in legal terms! This body functions not by rules, regulations and laws[5], but by the Spirit. In this it is vital for each**

[5] These are often disguised by calling them "principles." In doing that we cleverly cover the fact that we have simply added a human tradition as new law to be followed in the church.

member to hear the voice of the Lord and walk in the Spirit. In the body of Christ leadership has one task and one task only: to equip the saints for their task of ministry, which is best done by encouraging each member to hear the voice of God for himself or herself and respond in obedience. This is why the leaders in the early church were never 'settled pastors in churches overseeing programs,' but were itinerant leaders traveling with teams and ministering without taking ownership and control over people. They were servants bringing the message of Jesus in the power of the Spirit, as Paul wrote for example in Colossians 1:25-29: *I have become the servant of the church by the commission God gave me to present to you the word of God in its fullness – the mystery that has been kept hidden for ages and generations, but is now disclosed to the saints. To them God has chosen to make known among the Gentiles the glorious riches of this mystery, which is Christ in you, the hope of glory. We proclaim him, admonishing and teaching everyone with all wisdom, so that we may present everyone perfect in Christ. To this end I labor, struggling with all his energy, which so powerfully works in me.*

The real test of being the church is seen in the revelation of the very presence of Christ in us and the test of our leadership is seen in how those who have been touched by our ministry show forth the presence of the risen Lord through their lives. In the words of 2 Corinthians 2:14-3-6: *"But thanks be to God, who always leads us in triumphal procession in Christ and through us spreads everywhere the fragrance of the knowledge of him. For we are to God the aroma of Christ among those who are being saved and those who are perishing. To the one we are the smell of death; to the other the fragrance of life! And who is equal to such a task? Unlike so many, we do not peddle the word of God for profit. On the contrary, in Christ we speak before God in sincerity, like men sent from God.*

Are we beginning to commend ourselves again? Or do we need, like some people, letters of recommendation to you or from you? You yourselves are our letter, written on our hearts, known and read by everyone. You show you are a letter from Christ, the result of our ministry, written not with ink, but with the Spirit of the living God, not on tablets of stone, but on tablets of human hearts.

Such confidence as this is ours through Christ before God. Not that we are competent in ourselves to claim anything for ourselves, but our competence comes from God. He has made us competent as ministers of a new covenant – not of the letter, but of the Spirit: for the letter kills, but the Spirit gives life."

Let us consider this for a moment. In Christ we have received a new covenant which is not of the letter, but of the Spirit. This covenant is not about rules and regulations, but about hearing the Spirit and responding to his guidance. It is not about quoting Scripture and making rules based on Scripture (as the Pharisees did), but about revelation of Christ through the Spirit. Scripture without the presence and revelation of the Spirit brings death! This was exactly what happened with the Galatians. They started in freedom but the legalists derailed this and they turned back to the old principles and lost their freedom and their joy. The religious spirit brings bondage and gives birth to the slave children (Hagar) and the divine laughter (Isaac) is lost in the process, as Paul wrote in Galatians 4:21-31. Moreover, the children born in the natural will always persecute those born in the Spirit. They will put pressure on those walking in the Spirit to conform to the rules and regulations devised by the Levitical leaders and the keepers of the tradition. This brings us right back to the very beginning of this chapter, for the biggest challenge for those with a background in the Institutional Church is to learn to hear the Spirit and not to again submit to the bondage of the legalism in which we functioned for so long. In the words of Galatians 5:1: "*It is for freedom that Christ has set us free. Stand firm, then, and do not let yourself be burdened again by a yoke of slavery.*"

Thus, as we walk out of the world of the church, we often still carry the mindset of this world. In this we are struggling with this mindset just as the legalistic Jewish believers struggled with the issues of circumcision and other legalistic interpretations from the old covenant. It is very important to clearly hear the Spirit. Paul challenged the Galatians not to be trapped and try to fulfill the legal requirements of the old covenant by getting circumcised, for this would imply a return to seeking to become righteous through the law again (Galatians 5:2-6) and in the process fall from the grace given in Christ. Once free we have to stand in the freedom and walk in faith through the Spirit. In the words of Galatians 5:6: *For in Christ Jesus neither circumcision nor uncircumcision has any value. The only thing that counts is faith expressing itself through love.*

It is very important to note that the freedom given in Christ does not lead to lawlessness. Walking in the Spirit does not imply anarchy. One of the first reactions from those that have not walked in freedom and have the mindset of the world of the church is that the freedom offered will lead to total disorder and chaos. By using fear of 'what might happen' they try to discourage the freedom in the Spirit. In this process the letter that kills is used to discourage freedom and to institute order through a spirit of control. **The real issue is whether the church is a human organization or the body of the risen Lord led by the Spirit. Note again that according to the Scripture above the only thing that counts is faith expressing itself through love!** It is not in following rules and regulations that enforce a superficial order and uniformity, but in the unity of the Spirit which shows itself in each member serving the others that the law of God is fulfilled. The freedom offered in Christ is in the Spirit and it is not enforced through a system of rules and expectations overseen and judged by men and women, however holy and anointed they may be. It is vital to understand this and to change our mindsets if we want to remain free. This is precisely why Paul later in Galatians 5:13-15 says, *You, my brothers, were called to be free. But do not use your freedom to indulge in the sinful nature; rather, serve one another in love. The entire law is summed up in a single command: "Love your neighbor as yourself."*

The important question is this: "Do I trust the Spirit of the living God more than I trust any

person to guide me in truth and am I willing to live by his guidance, rather than by the advice and the opinion of any person?" To live by the Spirit is to trust him more than we trust any person. To live by the Spirit is to trust him to lead us in all truth. To live by the Spirit is to trust him to keep the order when we meet and to guide us in everything we need to do and say and minister. **Moreover, to live by the Spirit is the only way to be free and it is far more effective to keep us from sin than any rules and guidelines.** In the words of Colossians 2:23 *such regulations indeed have the appearance of wisdom, with their self-imposed worship, their false humility and their harsh treatment of the body, but they lack any value in restraining sensual indulgence.* However, if we *live by the Spirit we will not gratify the desires of the sinful nature,* as we read in Galatians 5:16. In fact, this is explained in more detail in verses 17-25: *For the sinful nature desires what is contrary to the Spirit, and the Spirit what is contrary to the sinful nature. They are in conflict with one another, so that you do not do what you want. But if you are led by the Spirit, you are not under the law. The acts of the sinful nature are obvious: sexual immorality; impurity and debauchery; idolatry and witchcraft; hatred, discord, jealousy, fits of rage, selfish ambition, dissensions, factions and envy; drunkenness, orgies, and the like. I warn you as I did before, that those who live like this will not inherit the kingdom of God. But the fruit of the Spirit is love, joy, peace, patience, kindness, goodness, faithfulness, gentleness and self-control. Against such things there is no law. Those who belong to Christ have crucified the sinful nature with its passions and desires. Since we live by the Spirit, let us keep in step with the Spirit.*

It is vital to grasp that living by the Spirit and keeping in step with the Spirit lead us into relationship with one another. That is what church is all about. It is not about meetings, buildings, programs, pastors and worship teams. It is about the practical relationships of the body. It is about each person becoming all that he/she is called to be in Christ and how we work together to encourage, support and build one another up. This is what caused Paul to be in the pain of childbirth again for the Galatians in order that Christ might be formed in them (Galatians 4:19). The very fruit of the Spirit described above had to become visible in the way they worked together. In fact, the passage above did not end with verse 25 above, but continued through Galatians 5:26-6:18 as follows:

Let us not become conceited, provoking and envying each other. Brothers, if someone is caught in a sin, you who are spiritual should restore him gently. But watch yourself, or you may also be tempted. Carry each other's burdens, and in this way you will fulfill the law of Christ. If anyone thinks he is something when he is nothing, he deceives himself. Each one should test his own actions. Then he can take pride in himself, without comparing himself to someone else, for each one should carry his own load.

Anyone who receives instruction in the word must share all good things with his instructor.

Do not be deceived: God cannot be mocked. A man reaps what he sows. The one who sows to please his sinful nature, from that nature will reap destruction; the one who sows to please the Spirit, from the Spirit will reap eternal life. Let us not become weary in doing good, for at the proper time we will reap a harvest if we do not give up. Therefore, as we have opportunity, let us do good to all people, especially to those who belong to the family of believers.

See what large letters I use as I write to you with my own hand. Those who want to make a good impression outwardly are trying to compel you to be circumcised. The only reason they do this is to avoid being persecuted for the cross of Christ. Not even those who are circumcised obey the law, yet they want you to be circumcised that they may boast about your flesh. May I never boast, except in the cross of our Lord, Jesus Christ, through which the world has been crucified to me and I to the world. Neither circumcision nor uncircumcision means anything; what counts is a new creation. Peace and mercy to all who follow this rule, even to the Israel of God.

Finally, let no one cause me trouble, for I bear on my body the marks of Jesus. The grace of our Lord Jesus Christ be with your spirit, brothers. Amen.

Real authentic church is about walking in the Spirit and is seen in the fruit of the Spirit made manifest in the relationships within the body. It is about caring for one another and bearing with one another, carrying one another's burdens. It is also about being responsible for one's own conduct and about being the member one is called to be in the body, being humble and expressing the fullness of Christ for the benefit of the body. This only comes through the Spirit and **what counts is a totally new creation.** The world and its ways and desires have been crucified with

Christ to bring forth this new creation. In the words of 2 Corinthians 5:14-20: *For Christ's love compels us, because we are convinced that one died for all and therefore all died. And he died for all that those who live should no longer live for themselves, but for him who died for them and was raised again. So from now on we regard no one from a worldly point of view. Though we once regarded Christ in this way, we do so no longer. Therefore, if anyone is in Christ, he is a new creation; the old has gone, the new has come. All this is from God who reconciled us to himself through Christ and gave us the ministry of reconciliation: that God was reconciling the world to himself in Christ, not counting men's sins against them. And he has committed to us the message of reconciliation. We are therefore Christ's ambassadors, as though God were making his appeal through us. We implore you on Christ's behalf: Be reconciled to God!*

In Christ we become a new creation. This is a spiritual creation and we are radically changed. We become compelled by the love of Christ and the way we see others is through the eyes of God's love given in Christ. The only thing that counts is our faith expressed in love toward one another. It is in us being the body of the risen Lord that God confronts the world with his reconciling love, as we demonstrate the power of reconciliation through love and forgiveness toward one another and toward those who reject the message and even persecute us. **Again, this has nothing to do with being an organization with officers, membership rules and expectations. It has everything to do with the fruit of the Spirit becoming visible in our relationships as members of the body of Christ**

as we serve one another. This is why Paul continued by writing the following in 2 Corinthians 6:1-10: *As God's fellow workers, we urge you not to receive God's grace in vain. For he says: "In the time of my favor I heard you and in the day of salvation I helped you." I tell you, now is the time of God's favor, now is the day of salvation."*

We put no stumbling block in anyone's path, so that our ministry will not be discredited. Rather, as servants of God we commend ourselves in every way: in great endurance; in troubles, hardships and distresses; in beatings, imprisonments and riots; in hard work, sleepless nights and hunger; in purity, understanding, patience and kindness; in the Holy Spirit and in sincere love; in truthful speech and in the power of God; with weapons of righteousness in the right hand and in the left; through glory and dishonor, bad report and good report; genuine, yet regarded as impostors; known, yet regarded as unknown; dying, and yet we live on; beaten, and yet not killed; sorrowful, yet always rejoicing; poor, yet making many rich; having nothing and yet possessing everything.

To sum this all up: As we walk in the Spirit, we learn to be the body of the risen Lord. We learn that it is neither to be driven by rules, expectations and leaders, nor to be motivated by guilt and fear or by rewards of human appreciation, but to be the members we are ordained to be in the body. It is not about doing, but about being! It is not about building or supporting an organization and programs, but about hearing the voice of God and responding in faith and obedience as he speaks, supporting and encouraging others. In this there is a freedom that the world of the church cannot offer.

However, as we step out from the slavery of the world of the church, we face the fact that we need to shed the mindset that kept us in bondage or we will fall right back. The first things that we had to deal with were the expectations and years of tradition around Sunday services.

FREEDOM FROM THE SUNDAY CHURCH PROGRAMS

When we began meeting with friends at the house, it happened to be that a weeknight was the best time. It worked! It could just as well have been on a Sunday morning, but a weeknight became our time to meet together with others. We will share more about this later, but two things happened in this regard that illustrate the power of the religious spirits and the pressure to fall back into bondage.

First, there were the 'concerned friends,' particularly from the fellowship that we had left. They wondered what happened and especially where we were fellowshipping. We simply replied that we meet with other believers at the house. However, invariably the question would come up: "Oh, but where do you go to church?" It is absolutely amazing how many cannot even consider the possibility of meeting as church outside of the walls of a building called a church with a sign advertising the church, pastor and service times. It may sound trivial to bring this up, but we have seen how this simple pressure can hinder and even enslave people. We have witnessed some who attend a house church and get healed from abuse, only to drift right back into a church with control and abuse, because they never really changed their mindset and never got the revelation of what the church of Christ is all about.

Second, there is the pressure of years of conditioning that really hits people when they move away from the Sunday Church programs. I can share that from personal experience. Church was a regular part of my week for fifty years. We were faithful and for many years I served as pastor. In fact, for me Sunday Church programs were central to my life. Strangely enough, even though I mentally knew what we were getting into and had no doubt about it in any way, I was not prepared for the emotional aspects that came with letting go of the Sunday Church baggage. It was so different to be relaxing at home on Sunday and getting used to the freedom to seek the Lord as family or individual – and to hear the Spirit say, "Relax!" At times guilt would hit, for we were not 'in church.' As I reflect on this, I also realize that going to church brought special rewards to the flesh in me. It made me feel good and by going I fulfilled the expectations of the other members. It also gave opportunities to minister publicly and gratified the need to be needed by others. After all, people are needed to run the programs like Sunday School, Bible

Study, etc. As the organization needs people to run the programs and to attend functions, many find a sense of self-worth in doing this. The religious spirits exploit this by tying one's identity to the support of the organization with the result that people may have no sense of relationship with God, but are loyal to the denomination or church. Walking away from this all is not unlike losing a job and the religious spirits will not easily give up. To walk away from the world of the church one has to face the temptation of seeking another religious position somewhere else, even if it is to be a loyal consumer in another church where you will be more than welcome, for they also 'need support.'

As we look at this it is very important to really grasp that church is not about an organization, but it is all about relationship in Christ. It is about being the church and walking and working in relationship with the other members of his body. Listen again to Colossians 2:16-23: *Therefore, do not let anyone judge you by what you eat or drink, or with regard to a religious festival, a New Moon celebration or a Sabbath Day. These are a shadow of the things that were to come; the reality however is found in Christ. Do not let anyone who delights in false humility and the worship of angels disqualify you for the prize. Such a person goes into great detail about what he has seen, and his unspiritual mind puffs him up with idle notions. He has lost connection with the head, from whom the whole body, supported and held together by its ligaments and sinews, grows as God causes it to grow. Since you have died with Christ to the basic principles of the world, why, as though you still belonged to it, do you submit to its rules: 'Do not handle! Do not taste! Do not touch!' These are destined to perish with use, because they are based on human commands and teachings. Such teachings indeed have an appearance of wisdom, with their self-imposed worship, their false humility and their harsh treatment of the body, but they lack any value in restraining sensual indulgence.*

As relationship is the key to being the church, it is important to meet with other believers on a regular basis. As we mentioned earlier, it happened that a weeknight was the best time for us to meet. Personally I like that immensely. By meeting on a weeknight, we have weekends to ourselves to rest, which is what the Sabbath was all about in the first place! In addition, we are free to travel, visit and do ministry where the Lord leads us. A weeknight also opens the door for those who are in an Institutional Church to explore what house church is all about, without having to immediately let go of the traditional service. More importantly, being free on Sunday mornings especially opens the door to evangelism, for example by going for a walk you will meet those who are not in church! We know others who were led (or chose) to meet as house church on Sunday mornings. There is no rule for or against this. **The important thing is to get together with other believers on a regular basis and to build and strengthen relationships and encourage one another.**

At this point there is more baggage to handle and to let go. Again, years of Institutional Church programs will hinder the body to function as it should. **It is not about**

becoming a small version of the Institutional Church meeting at a house, but about learning to function as body. Many think house church is simply another church meeting at a house. Thus, the first expectation is that there has to be a "pastor" to preach and run the program. In fact, some miss the whole experience, because they do not feel equipped to preach or teach and never step out into the call of God for their lives! **The world of the western church has been fixated on the sermon[6] as the key reason to meet on Sunday. The preaching of the Word is expected to be in the form of a well-reasoned message showing the academic abilities of the preacher to research the topic and deliver the message.** Very few people grasp the fact that this is simply cultural baggage in a religious package. The Greek words for preaching in the New Testament are *keruso* and *euangello.* The first is the announcement of the kingdom of God and the second the preaching of the Good News (gospel). **In Scripture both of these words are exclusively linked to the preaching of the gospel to unbelievers! Preaching was not for believers. Those who responded by accepting the message of the Good News became members of the body and were taught**

6 Former pagan orators brought sermons into the church in the beginning of the 3rd century. (See Mega Shift by James Rutz, p221). This is in a chapter outlining the history of the slide of the church from organism to organization. Frank Viola traces the pagan origins of our many church traditions in a well-researched and detailed work, "Pagan Christianity: The origins of our modern church practices".

the basics of the faith, which meant they learned to walk in the Way. Again, they were not taught through pastors preaching sermons. Teaching took place in an interactive way through discussion and dialog, usually in local home. In Acts 20:7-12 we find an excellent example where Paul spoke and talked at length. Reading this passage in the English it may be misunderstood as a lengthy monologue, but the Greek word is the word 'dialog.' Paul did not preach, but led the discussion, which was open to everyone. This is the background to 1 Corinthians 14:26: *What then shall we say, brothers? When you come together, everyone has a hymn, a word of instruction, a revelation, a tongue or an interpretation.* Teaching involves everyone as the Spirit leads and must build the whole body. The one-way sermon as applied in the church today was not found in the early church and it elevates one member, the Pastor/preacher to a position that was never ordained by our Lord. It effectively denies opportunity for the whole body to function as body and contribute to the welfare of the members.

Having said that, it is baggage that many carry into the house church as they move out of the Institutional Church. It becomes even more difficult because most adult fellowship groups in the Institutional Church are built around 'teaching and training' or 'Bible Studies.' Thus, we found that some that came to the house church expected that there will not only be preaching, but that it would be central. In addition, they expected that this teaching or preaching would be in the style they used to have in the Institutional Church with 'a teacher on a podium speaking forth the message for those in attendance.' **Our Institutionalized mindsets have made Jesus into a western pastor with a podium preaching to the crowds or teaching in a classroom. We have sterilized the stories in the gospels so that most see Jesus as a 'pastor in a pulpit' – even when he sat down at the well, walked down the street, entered Jerusalem, healed the sick, etc. Somehow most people expect that when they gather in a house or church building, Jesus and the Holy Spirit really show up 'when the Word is being preached!' The revelation that Jesus, the hope of glory, is in each one and reveals himself in and through each person is of the utmost importance, but to see that we need to shed the baggage of the Pastor/preacher with the sermon. The issue we face is the model of western teaching, which is based on a monologue with passive listeners. We need to let go of that and meet the risen Lord as he reveals himself in and through the members of his body when they meet in his name. It is in the relationship of loving care for one another that most lessons are taught and learned. It happens around the table where we eat and talk, just like it did in the home of Martha and Mary and the houses of Zacchaeus and Simon, the Pharisee. It happens when a need is revealed (even at an inopportune time, like the lady with the issue of blood secretly**

trying to touch Jesus) and all stop to minister to the person in need. It happens when a little child interrupts the adult conversation and Jesus turns his focus away from the 'mature members' to bless a child – and the least becomes the example of Kingdom living.

It is amazing to see the stifling effect of the mindsets of people walking out of the Institutional Church regarding this matter. It is as if the truth often cannot penetrate the mindsets to bring freedom from the classroom expectations with which most of us have been raised. It requires a major paradigm shift to let go of this baggage and to learn to be the body through love and care, growing in relationship. It takes time to learn and experience that teaching is best done interactively with all members involved. It takes revelation to know that the Holy Spirit is the best teacher and "*the anointing we received from him remains in us and we do not need anyone to teach us,*" as John wrote in 1 John 2:27. This is why Jesus said to his disciples in John 14:25-26: "*All this I have spoken while still with you. But the Counselor, the Holy Spirit whom the Father will send in my name, will teach you all things and will remind you of everything I have said to you.*" It is in the process of doing the work of ministry in faith under the anointing (the powerful presence of the Spirit) that we learn most effectively. In fact, it was precisely in walking out their faith, that the 72 sent out learned that even demons had to submit to them in the name of Jesus and the Father revealed these truths to little children, while hiding it from the wise and learned. In the same way ordinary people learn that they are anointed and appointed as royal priests and empowered to do greater works than Jesus, as he said in John 14:12, when they meet in his name and encourage and build one another up and minister in his name. It is in ministering to one another and honoring and encouraging one another as members that we learn to function as one body and begin to grow in faith and witness. In Romans 15:14 Paul wrote the following **to all in Rome** (many of whom were uneducated slaves, but loved and called by God according to Romans 1:7 and thus members of the body): *"I myself am convinced, my brothers, that you yourselves are full of goodness, complete in knowledge and competent to instruct one another."*

Before we move on to the freedom and privilege to minister in the Spirit, we need to make some brief comments about the other programs which also hinder and trip God's people as they walk out of the world of the church into the freedom of the Spirit. It is very revealing that when the 72 returned from their mission Jesus remarked that the Father hid these things from the wise and learned and revealed them to little children (Luke 10:21). On another occasion the disciples tried to keep the mothers from bringing their children to Jesus so that he could touch them – and Jesus rebuked them. In fact, he plainly told them that unless they become like little children, they would not enter the Kingdom! **Interestingly enough, this very passage has become the foundation of the Sunday school programs that remove**

children from the communion of the saints to teach them (western style) about Jesus. We have substituted PROGRAM for relationship and can literally quote the very words of Jesus against the removal of the children from the adults out of context to lay the foundations of the very programs that take them away from the place where 'the adults meet Jesus!' Thus, we offer PROGRAMS instead of allowing the children to be built on Christ (the stone rejected by men) as living stones into a spiritual house to become with us in the unity of the Spirit a holy priesthood, offering spiritual sacrifices acceptable to God through Jesus Christ. In this we are no different than the keepers of the temple and its traditions who were upset when Jesus entered Jerusalem and cleansed the temple. They were indignant, so Matthew recorded in Matthew 21:15, when the children loudly praised God and shouted "Hosanna to the Son of David" as they saw the blind and the lame coming to Jesus in the temple to be healed. The controllers of the world of religious tradition were upset with the children. When God interrupted the program that they controlled, they did not even recognize him, but the Father revealed this to the little ones! The wise and learned did not see the divine presence in Jesus, for they were more concerned with their positions and power and keeping order and missed the visitation of God. Jesus' response is even more revealing, for he asked them if they ever read Psalm 8:2, "From the lips of children and infants you have ordained praise." Incidentally, this verse further says that this praise actually shuts the mouth of Satan and his demonic forces.

So, with our worldly wisdom we choose programs over relationship and remove the most effective spiritual weapon from our midst, so that our 'adult program' will be 'dignified' and without the disruption of children. In doing this we open the door for the spirits of division and cut the body of the Lord into pieces and stuff them in different parts of the building, reserving 'the sanctuary' for the adults to pay homage to the local priests and their attending Levites overseeing and managing the religious program. To add to all of this, the Sunday school program needs to be managed and so a whole bureaucracy is invented and with it some "gifts" not found in Scripture are discovered. So we have those with gifts to work with children and with youth to become teachers and youth pastors. Their task is to prepare the young ones to serve the system and be the future managers and keepers of tradition – local and more importantly denominational. Thus, they need to know what sets their church apart from the other churches and what are the key doctrinal 'truths' that separate them from the other churches. **It is no wonder that the vast majority of the children that graduate from these programs do not stay in the church once they leave home. Those who do remain in the church often have no personal relationship with Jesus, for they were taught**

how to be religious through supporting and maintaining the institutional programs. In a word, some move away from the church into the world without faith and most who stay function in the world of the church supporting their particular brand of corporate religion. The very programs designed and intended to bring the children and youth to faith are often the biggest stumbling block to the truth, for truth is not found in a program however well designed and intended, but it is found in an authentic relationship with the Truth, Jesus.

There is more institutional baggage yet, especially the general concept of worship. I had not seen this until it became very evident through a comment by a friend. They led a house church for some time and then returned to the institutional church "joining" a small church. This church in reality is very close to a house church, but functions in an institutional way with a special building, staff and programs. The comment my friend made was that he had really missed "corporate worship" in the house church. By "corporate worship" he meant a larger group singing hymns and/or spiritual songs mostly with instrumental accompaniment. To most if not all raised in the institutional church that is what "corporate worship" is, even though there are major differences depending on the traditions and denomination to which one belongs, e. g. the music styles, choirs or worship teams, types of instruments and whether or not dancing with or without flags and banners is acceptable.

Thus, **to most "church people" worship implies the singing of hymns and spiritual songs led by appointed leaders usually with musical accompaniment.** What makes it corporate is that it takes place at a corporate gathering of the members in the church building joining together in the worship. One is tempted to wonder how many members are needed to make it true corporate worship, e. g. if only the pastor shows up or the organist, can there be true corporate worship? One might even take it a step further like the joke about changing a light bulb and ask how many members of each denomination are needed to have true corporate worship. The point is that if the size of the group does not matter then surely one can have meaningful corporate worship in any venue. However, more important to the discussion is the question as to what Christian worship is and for that we need to go to the Scriptures.

The first thing we note is that the New Testament has very little to say about worship when defined in terms of music and song. In the gospels we find only one reference to Jesus and the disciples singing, as we read in Matthew 26:13 that following the Passover and the Last Supper, *when they had sung a hymn, they went out to the Mount of Olives.* In the Book of Acts the only reference we have is in chapter 16:25 where we read that Paul and Silas were praying and singing hymns at midnight when they were in prison. In the Book of Revelation there are pictures of worship in heaven which include singing, but these are not pictures of the church on earth. That leaves the New Testament letters where we find a couple of references to individual singing (1 Cor. 14:15 and James 5:13) as well as three references to music and songs in a corporate setting. In Col. 3 we find guidelines for Christian conduct and it includes the following words in verses 16-17: *Let the word of Christ dwell in you richly as you teach and admonish one another with all wisdom, and as you sing psalms, hymns and spiritual songs with gratitude in your hearts to God. And whatever you do, whether in word or in deed, do it all in the name of the Lord Jesus, giving thanks to God the Father through him.* In a very similar context Eph. 5:19-20 states: *Speak to one another with psalms, hymns and spiritual songs. Sing and make music in your hearts to the Lord, always giving thanks to God the Father for everything, in the name of our Lord Jesus Christ.* It is interesting to note that the music and singing was to be both to God and to one another. This ties in with the guidelines for corporate gatherings of believers in 1 Cor. 14:26: *What then shall we say, brothers? When you come together, everyone has a hymn, or a word of instruction, a revelation, a tongue or an interpretation. All of these must be done for the strengthening of the church.* We will look at these again, but for now note that the corporate aspect of everything that takes place when we gather has to do with the strengthening of the church as we minister to one another.

However we want to read the New Testament, there is very little if anything upon which we can base the generally accepted idea of worship to be predominantly seen as songs sung in a gathering under the appointed leadership. There is a very clear definition of true worship in the New Testament, but it includes much more than the above. We will look at that shortly, but first have to note something else. With the lack of evidence to substantiate the general understanding and practice of worship in our churches from the New Testament, most turn to the Old Testament. There is indeed a wealth of information upon which to base a theology of worship as practiced in the churches. However, there is 'a small problem' in that it is all part and parcel of the Levitical system of the old covenant, with a special caste of leaders overseeing and managing the process! The letter to the Hebrews makes it abundantly clear that this whole system was abolished in Christ and that it had become obsolete, e. g. Hebrews 8:13: *By calling this covenant "new," he has made the first obsolete; and what is obsolete and aging will soon disappear.* **Please note that it is not to say we are not to sing and worship and no one can lead in a song. It does mean, however, that the whole hierarchical structure that elevates a special group to function like the Levitical leadership of the Old Testament, even when using new terminology like worship leaders, is not the model of the church as we shall see in the next chapter.** Moreover, even in the Old Testament it was recognized that corporate gatherings with music and song do not necessarily mean true worship. Thus Amos 5:21 – 24 reads:

I hate, I despise your religious feasts;
I cannot stand your assemblies.
Even though you bring me burnt offerings and grain offerings,
I will not accept them.
Though you bring choice fellowship offerings,
I have no regard for them.
Away with the noise of your songs!
I will not listen to the music of your harps.
But let justice roll like a river,
Righteousness like a never-failing stream!

True worship flows from a heart in tune with God's heart, manifesting in the expression of a Kingdom lifestyle. Without that it is meaningless. Even the most beautiful music and songs by the most accomplished musicians and singers are worthless if their lives do not show the fruit of the Kingdom life first and foremost made manifest in Christ. This is very clearly expressed in Romans 12:1-2 where worship is defined: *Therefore, I urge you, brothers, in view of God's mercy, to offer your bodies as living sacrifices, holy and pleasing to God – this is your spiritual act of worship. Do not conform any longer to the pattern of this world, but be transformed by the renewing of your mind. Then you will be able to test and approve what God's will is – his good pleasing and perfect will.*

Therefore, worship in the New Covenant sense of the word is much more than music and song! It covers all of life and is a response of gratitude to God for his gift of life in full to us in Christ. It becomes true corporate worship when we recognize our corporate nature as body of Christ and respond by laying down our lives for him and for one another as members of his body, as outlined in the passages that follow the quote above in Romans 12:3-21. The greatest act of corporate worship took place when one man, Jesus Christ, honored the Father by laying down his life on the cross to make it possible for people like us to become members of his body! As we saw in the Scriptures above, when the believers gathered, they had music and they sang together as part of their worship, but they did much more! They encouraged one another, prophesied to one another, ministered to each other, prayed for one another, etc. Once we recognize this, we understand that true corporate worship is often best expressed in a small intimate setting. It is not about how many sing the same song at the same time, however great it is to do that! In fact, I am blessed to be married to a wonderful lady who has a heart for worship and loves to dance, often with flags. I have witnessed as she put a CD on and danced and prayed for needs in the nation or community or church. In a real sense this is as much corporate worship as a gathering of thousands in an auditorium, for in doing this she literally offered her body as a living sacrifice for the sake of the body of our Lord.

We can also look at this from another angle. In John 4 Jesus met a Samaritan lady at the well and as the discussion developed, she asked his opinion on where they were to worship, i.e. whether the Jews or the Samaritans had it right. Jesus answered that a time was coming when worship would not be confined to a specific locality, but *a time is coming and has now come when the true worshipers will worship the Father in Spirit and in truth, for they are the kind of worshipers the Father seeks. God is Spirit and his worshipers must worship in Spirit and in truth (John 4:23-24)*. True worship involves all of life and how we live. As we open ourselves to the Spirit and respond to his guidance in meeting the needs of others wherever they may be, willing to sacrifice as needed, we honor our Lord and worship the Father. Understanding of what true worship is frees one from the traditional baggage to enjoy the full experience of worship including music and song in whatever setting one may be.

As we walked out of the corporate world of the institutionalized western church, the whole program approach had to be shed including the divisions caused by this corporate mindset, from denominational to hierarchical, racial, gender and age. We had to learn how to walk in the Spirit and how to include and appreciate each member, loving one another and building one another up. We had to learn to release one another, including the little ones, whether little in faith or little in stature. We had to learn to trust the Spirit to work in and through each member, regardless of the person. We had to commit to paying the price to function as the body of Christ and to live, speak and act in relationship where the presence of the Spirit is confirmed by the fruit of the Spirit showing forth in the way we relate to one another. It does not come easy for most, as there is so much baggage to be shed. In fact, most of us do not realize how tired and heavily burdened we are with all the religious baggage, until we begin to shed this and take the yoke of Christ and find the rest only he can offer. In the process we are set free to be who we are and to allow others to be who they are and work together to express our faith in the unity in the Spirit. Paying the price of commitment to relationship we grow corporately and as individuals, and we recover the joy of childhood in God's family. As we shift the attention away from programs to relationships, we discover that the church is neither a place nor an organization, but it is the body of the Christ who lives in each member. Expressing the unity of our relationship in the Spirit we are the church and it opens the door to being the church wherever we are and whenever we meet together in his name. **It is not about preaching and teaching these truths, but about living it every day and expressing this in the way we relate to others. It is learning to walk in the freedom of the Spirit and in trusting him to guide us whenever and wherever we meet with one another! It is about shedding the religious baggage and controls and trusting Jesus to be the head and to lead us through the Spirit in everything. It brings about a lightness and a joy to leadership who are set free from the need to control in order to serve as the Spirit leads and to release people to become children and express their faith in action as they minister to one another.**

FREEDOM TO BECOME A SERVANT

As we walked out of the world of the church there was a radical adjustment needed in our mindsets regarding ministry. On a personal level I was trained and ordained to serve in a Levitical system and then found myself walking away from it into the freedom of the order of Melchizedek. Instead of overseeing and controlling the programs and people, I needed to release my control to the Holy Spirit. Instead of being in charge, I had to truly submit to the Spirit and allow him to lead. I had to learn to trust him to speak to the body through even the least likely member. This is more than an academic exercise! Even though I grew up in a way that allowed me to easily release people and delegate authority, I still had to learn to let go of my need to control. In addition, there were the expectations of others trained in the system urging me to 'exercise leadership,' thus insisting that I take control in the worldly sense of playing the role of pastor yet again. As we noted earlier, it is difficult for former slaves to exercise their rights and freedoms. Likewise, it is difficult for slave drivers to let go of the spirit of control. In fact, as we began the journey, my roots in the old Levitical system showed up in a powerful way. In truth, I had cut the tree down, but the roots were still there! Within a short time, I had the plan down on paper and was ready to begin building a network of house churches! The old roots were beginning to sprout a new system of 'inter-dependent' house churches where I would serve as the coordinator and overseer. After all, someone needed to manage and oversee these churches and I was anointed as leader. As I see the Spirit moving in the western world and God beginning to shake the heavens and the earth revealing the cracked foundations of the church and setting the stage for the restoration of his church, I also see how these old roots again try to sprout. Many in the current house church movement have not yet dealt with the spirit of control and the new plant is often but a disguised sprout of the old roots. **In his grace God forced me into a place of brokenness and inability to pursue my plans as I had intended at the time. Instead, we were forced to stay an insignificant little group meeting in our home (at times only us as a couple!) and learning the truth in humility. God was more interested in getting the old roots out of my life than joining me in my big ambition to launch the house church network for his glory.** It was like Joshua who found that the angel of the Lord was neither for nor against them. Joshua had to submit to the angel as the commander in the battle, as we read in Joshua 5:13ff.

Ultimately God is building his church. Jesus said this to the disciples in Matthew 16:17-19. The church is built only on the rock, which is Jesus himself, as the Messiah, the Son of thc living God. As we come to him, the living stone - rejected by men but chosen by God and precious to him – we also are being built like living stones into a spiritual house to be a holy priesthood offering spiritual sacrifices acceptable to God through Jesus Christ. He is the one handling the living stones and making them fit into this building, the church. He is the one shaping each stone and placing it where he chooses! Like me, some need to be shaped in ways they never expected and the master builder has to chip some rough edges off and remove some imperfections! Like a true stone mason, he will fit a bump in my life to fill a hole in another so that a strong bond is formed, thereby putting me with someone who thinks and acts in a way that is very different from my ways. Yes, he stretches us every day through others! I had to learn that the Spirit was far more able to lead and direct the body than I could ever be! I needed to trust him to lead his church and I needed to be delivered of the spirit of control. I had to learn that he really meant it when hc told his disciples that those who want to be great in the kingdom had to become servants. It is very sobering to really read what Jesus said in this regard as recorded in Matthew 20:25-28, *"You know that the rulers of the Gentiles lord it over them, <u>and their high</u>*

officials exercise authority over them. Not so with you! Instead, whoever wants to become great among you must be your servant, and whoever wants to be first must be your slave – just as the Son of man did not come to be served, but to serve, and to give his life as a ransom for many." To be a leader in the Kingdom one has to let go the idea of exercising authority over others! True Kingdom authority is released to those who choose to serve and through their service build relationships that open the door to speak into people's lives in love, especially when correction is needed. This is beautifully illustrated in the life and words of Paul to the Corinthians when he challenged them and pleaded with them in his letter. At the end wrote these words in 2 Corinthians 13:10, *"This is why I write these things when I am absent, that when I come I may not have to be harsh in my use of authority – the authority the Lord gave me for building you up, not for tearing you down."* We have personally ministered to far too many who have been ripped apart and torn down by 'men and women in authority.' The prophetic words of Ezekiel 34 have become very relevant in this day and age in the western church where we have chosen to reject the order of Melchizedek and replaced it with a worldly Levitical system.

As I laid down my life and my ambitions, however spiritual they were, I had to learn to serve by allowing and helping others walk in freedom. This included setting the captives free – whether they were former Levites that needed deliverance from spirits of control or former slaves that needed to learn to walk in freedom and exercise their ministry in the priesthood of the believers. In letting go of my life, the life of the resurrected Christ was released in me. In laying my ambitions on the altar, the Kingdom vision was revealed to me. In sacrificing my authority, the authority of the Spirit began to manifest as I dealt with others. In letting go of my hold on 'my possessions' I learned to trust the Father for provision and he really worked to smooth the rough edges on this in my life! In letting go of the worldly model of leadership and becoming a servant, I learned to trust the Spirit to lead and his fruit began to show more in my life and I became more effective in ministry.

When I chose not to be purpose driven, I was set free to be Spirit led! I stepped off the religious treadmill designed to run the same old same old year-round unproductive programs and away from the futility of trying to meet people's expectations. Like the Samaritan woman at the well, I found the one who offered me living water to quench the thirst. It tasted so different than the "holy water" poured from the religious buckets of some "big-name leader's" anointing which I (and so many others) sought to quench the thirst. I came to the waters, tired and burdened by religion and its load, and he gave me a drink. As I drank a river of living water was released from my innermost being and the burdens lifted and healing flowed through my body and soul. His yoke was placed upon my shoulders, but it was

so much lighter than the religious burdens of the world of the church. I learned from him and discovered he was indeed gentle and humble in heart and I found rest for my soul. My eyes were opened to the simplicity of the church as the body of Jesus. As this happened, the Spirit helped me to see others and myself through his eyes. The best way to explain this is to look at two passages of Scripture, 2 Corinthians 5 and Romans 12.

It is important to look at 2 Corinthians 5 in the context of the whole letter so bear with me as we lay these foundations. Paul had intended to visit the church in Corinth as he traveled to Macedonia and again a second time on his return from there. However, he changed his mind because of some painful issues that he wanted to have resolved before he came in person. This letter was written to resolve the issues and to restore the relationship between them. That relationship began as he laid the foundations of the church by preaching the good news of Jesus to them and followed it up by pouring his life into those who had accepted the gospel. He became a spiritual father to them. However, once the foundations were laid, he released the ministry to them and left. This letter is a powerful example of spiritual leadership by the apostle who laid the foundations of the church. Rather than abusing his authority like the false apostles to lord it over them and use them for personal gain, he walked in humility, seeking to build them up rather than pull them down. In fact, he pleaded with them on the basis of his relationship with them, which was established in love and expressed in servant hood.

With that background, let us look at the main themes leading to 2 Corinthians 5. In the opening chapter Paul explained why he changed his mind about the planned visits and how he chose to forgive the offender so that Satan's schemes would not work. Then he moved on to writing about the fact that they, being believers, are ministers of the New Covenant:

Unlike so many, we do not peddle the word of God for profit. On the contrary, in Christ we speak before God with sincerity, like men sent from God. Are we beginning to commend ourselves again? Or do we need, like some people, letters of recommendation to you or from you? You show that you are a letter from Christ, the result of our ministry, written not with ink, but with the Spirit of the living God, not on tablets of stone, but on tablets of human hearts. Such confidence as this is ours through Christ before God. Not that we are competent in ourselves to claim anything for ourselves, but our competence comes from God. He has made us competent as ministers of a new covenant – not of the letter, but of the Spirit; for the letter kills, but the Spirit gives life.

Let us note a few key points here: Paul's apostolic ministry (men sent from God) resulted in a church functioning in the Spirit without a resident 'pastor' to oversee and run the programs. Further, Paul did not remain to pastor this church (or any of the other churches he planted) nor did he make sure that there was a resident pastor appointed or chosen. Paul also did not minister for personal gain and did not receive a salary from this church, even when he was actively doing the work of ministry in Corinth. He simply laid the foundations and once the church was established, he moved on with his team. The task of the apostle was to walk in the Spirit and share the message of the New Covenant with the competence given by God. The New Covenant is of the Spirit. He gives life as the living water is released from the innermost being of each member and this is far more glorious than the Old Covenant as we read in 2 Corinthians 3:7-16. The New Covenant releases the members of the church into the freedom of the Spirit where each one becomes a minister in the order of Melchizedek and becomes transformed into the likeness of Jesus, as Paul wrote in 2 Corinthians 3:17-18:

Now the Lord is the Spirit and where the Spirit of the Lord is, there is freedom. And we, who with unveiled faces all reflect the glory of the Lord, are being transformed into his likeness with ever-increasing glory, which comes from the Lord, who is the Spirit.

True leadership is simply to become a servant to the others to set them free to follow the guidance of the Spirit in ministry. Once people know the Lord personally and are filled with the Spirit, they need to be released in full to walk in the Spirit. There is a point – and it does not take years and years of studies and control – where they have to be released to ministry in the body. This is why there is to be no one person, whether called 'pastor' or 'apostle' or by any other title, managing the church, that is the body of believers. It is true that some individuals will play an important role in the lives of many in a certain locality or house at certain times, but when they continue to be seen as more important or more spiritual or more anointed than the others, it holds the members back in their spiritual growth. Spiritual leadership must be focused on releasing the members as soon as possible and moving on, trusting that the Spirit is more able to lead and direct the church than any human being. True leadership will set the others free, much like it happens in a family: There is a time when we release our children and even though we remain the parents, our roles change. They have the choice to seek our advice or reject it. They have the choice to walk in relationship or break it. Like the father in the parable of the prodigal son, our task as spiritual fathers and mothers is to simply love our children – all of them – without controlling their lives.

This is exactly what Paul did with the Corinthians (and with the other churches he planted). In his own words in 1 Corinthians 4:15-16 he said: *"Even though you have ten thousand guardians in Christ, you do not have many fathers, for in Christ Jesus I became your father through the gospel. Therefore I urge you to imitate me."* His father's heart is further illustrated in the way he continued to deal with them at the point when they had chosen to follow false leaders and some rejected him. He continued to be a servant and pleaded with them on the basis of his relationship as spiritual father as we read in 2 Corinthians 7:2-4: *Make room for us in your hearts. We have wronged no one, we have corrupted no one, we have exploited no one. I do not say this to condemn you; I have said before that you have such a place in our hearts that we would live or die with you. I have great confidence in you; I take great pride in you. I am greatly encouraged; in all our troubles, my joy knows no bounds.*

The ministry of the New Covenant flows out of a heart of love with a willingness to set people free even when it hurts. In fact, it often does, as Paul found with the Corinthians. The key to handling this is to know that this ministry is from the Lord and with it we receive his mercy to help us in times of hurt, pain and rejection. It is not about us, but about Jesus who was the living stone rejected by men! The amazing thing is that as we walk through such tough times, the presence of the Spirit enables us to show forth the power of God in our lives. This is set forth in 2 Corinthians 4:1-12 in the following words: *Therefore, since through God's mercy we have this ministry, we do not lose heart. Rather, we have renounced secret and shameful ways; we do not use deception, nor do we distort the word of God. On the contrary, by setting forth the truth plainly we commend ourselves to every man's conscience. And even if our gospel is veiled, it is veiled to those who are perishing. The god of this age has blinded the minds of unbelievers, so that they cannot see the light of the gospel of the glory of Christ, who is the image of God. For we do not preach ourselves, but Jesus Christ as Lord, and ourselves as servants for Jesus' sake. For God who said, "Let light shine out of darkness," made his light shine in our hearts to give us the light of the glory of God in the face of Christ. But we have this treasure in jars of clay. To show that this all surpassing power is from God and not from us, we are hard pressed on every side, but not crushed; perplexed, but not in despair; persecuted, but not abandoned; struck down, but not destroyed. We always carry around in our body the death of Jesus, so that the life of Jesus may also be revealed in our body. For we who are alive are always being given over to death for Jesus' sake, so that his life may be revealed in our mortal body. So then, death is at work in us, but life is at work in you.*

To be a leader in the church is to become a servant and it has a huge price tag. It means to be willing to become vulnerable and to suffer rejection and misunderstanding. The all-surpassing power of God is revealed in the way we respond to the suffering we undergo. This is a far cry from the 'religious' view of many in institutional churches seeking the power in positions, titles and in their 'anointed ministry' that opens the way to be on the platforms and in the limelight. From the platform we see a sea of faces and miss the detail. It gives a sense of power looking down on the masses and it feeds the ego, but we miss relationship. However, becoming vulnerable as a servant and in humility considering others better than ourselves, we learn to walk as Jesus did and to lead as he led. This is exactly what Paul experienced time and again, as we read for example in Philippians 1:27-2:11 and as we read this, remember that he wrote this while imprisoned for his faith: *Whatever happens, conduct yourselves in a manner worthy of the gospel of Christ. Then, whether I come and see you or hear about you in my absence, I will know that you stand firm in one spirit, contending as one man for the faith of the gospel without being frightened in any way by those who oppose you. This is a sign to them that they will be* *destroyed, but that you will be saved – and that by God. For it has been granted to you on behalf of Christ not only to believe on him, but also to suffer for him, since you are going through the same struggle you saw I had and now hear that I still have. If you have any encouragement from being united with Christ, if any comfort from his love, if any fellowship with the Spirit, if any tenderness and compassion, then make my joy complete by being like-minded, having the same love, being one in spirit and in purpose. Do nothing out of selfish ambition or vain conceit, but in humility consider others better than yourselves. Each of you should look not only to your own interests, but also to the interests of others. Your attitude should be the same as that of Christ Jesus:*

Who, being in the very nature of God,
did not consider equality with God something to be grasped,
but made himself nothing,
taking the very nature of a slave, being made in human likeness,
And being found in the appearance as a man,
he humbled himself and became obedient to death – even death on a cross.
Therefore God exalted him to the highest place
and gave him the name that is above every name,
that at the name of Jesus every knee should bow,
in heaven and on earth and under the earth,
and every tongue confess that Jesus Christ is Lord,
to the glory of God the Father.

The door to spiritual leadership in the church is to walk in the footsteps of Christ and become a servant. It is not how many people are under you and looking up to you, but how many people you lift up to the Lord. It is not how many people submit to you and call you 'Pastor,' but how many people are set free to walk in the Spirit. It is not how powerful you move in the Spirit, *for many will say, "Lord, Lord, did we not prophesy in your name and in your name drive out demons and perform many miracles," and Jesus will tell them plainly, "I never knew you! Away from me, you evildoers!"* (Matthew 7:22-23). It is about the fruit of the Spirit, for by the fruit you will recognize them (Matthew 7: 15-20). **The fruit of true leadership is the humility to consider others better than ourselves and to look out for their interests. Leadership is revealed in the willingness to die of self for the sake of others.** With this established, let us return to 2 Corinthians 4 where we left off and read verses 12-18: *So then, death is at work in us, but life is at work in you. It is written: "I believed; therefore I have spoken." With that same spirit of faith we also believe and therefore speak, because we know that the one who raised Jesus from the dead will also raise us with Jesus and present us with you in his presence. All this is for your benefit, so that the grace that is reaching more and more people may cause thanksgiving to overflow to the glory of God. Therefore, we do not loose heart. Though outwardly we are wasting away, yet inwardly we are being renewed day by day. For our light and momentary problems are achieving for us an eternal glory that far outweighs them all. So we fix our eyes not on what is seen, but on what is unseen. For what is seen is temporary, but what is unseen is eternal.* Following this Paul points to the fact that our mortal bodies are a temporary dwelling and will be replaced by an eternal body. Even though we long to be in the eternal body, we live in this mortal body with the confidence that we have an eternal destiny and we live by faith and not by sight, as we read in 2 Corinthians 5:5-7: *Now it is God who made us for this very purpose and has given us the Spirit as a deposit, guaranteeing what is to come. Therefore we are always confident and know that as long as we are at home in the body we are away from the Lord. We live by faith, not by sight.*

This is the key issue: We live by faith and not by sight. We see things from a very different perspective, for we are seated with Christ in heavenly places. We look at life through Kingdom eyes and walk in Kingdom authority with a Kingdom vision. This means that we seek to please the King, for we are accountable to him and him alone! At the same time there has to be a transparency in our lives so that others see the presence of Christ in us. In the words of 2 Corinthians 5:7-11, *we live by faith, not by sight. We are confident, I say, and would prefer to be away from the body and at home with the Lord. So we make it our goal to please him, whether we are at home in the body or away from it. For we must all appear before the judgment seat of Christ, that each one may receive what is due him for the things done while in the body, whether good or bad. Since we know then what it is to fear the Lord, we try to persuade men. What we are is plain to God, and I hope it is also plain to your conscience.*

Living by faith means that we not only see things from a different perspective, but as leaders we look at others through very different eyes, as we read in 2 Corinthians 5:16-17: *So then,* *we regard no one from a worldly point of view. Though we once regarded Christ in this way, we do so no longer. Therefore, if anyone is in Christ, he is a new creation: the old has gone, the new has come!* As leaders we look at people through the eyes of Christ. We look past their humanity to see the divine potential in them. A person's divine potential is best seen in recognizing him or her as part of the body of the risen Lord, in whom he/she becomes a new creation. **My task as a leader is to spiritually discern the potential of another person in Christ and to become a servant to develop and release that potential as fully as possible so that the person will serve as royal priest in the order of Melchizedek.** In the words of Ephesians 4:11-13 *Jesus gave some to be apostles, some to be prophets, some to be evangelists and some to be pastors and teachers, to prepare God's people for works of service, so that the body of Christ may be built up until we all reach unity in the faith and knowledge of the Son of God and become mature, reaching to the whole measure of the fullness of Christ.* This has nothing to do with being a local pastor (by whatever title) running a program and identifying 'the gifts of the members' to serve the local church's programs. In fact, this is very evident when we look at Romans 12, which is another passage about the church as body of Christ.

Let us set the stage by reading Romans 12:1-2: *Therefore, I urge you, brothers, in view of God's mercy, to offer your bodies as living sacrifices, holy and pleasing to God – this is your spiritual act of worship. Do not conform any longer to the pattern of this world, but be transformed through the renewal of your mind.*

Then you will be able to test and approve what God's will is – his good and pleasing and perfect will. Our lives in Christ are in response to God's mercy shown to us! It calls for a radical laying down of our lives as living sacrifices. This brings about a radical change in mindset and a breaking with the pattern of the world. **This is why the current leadership model in the church cannot be maintained with integrity, for it is the very opposite of the servant hood modeled by Jesus. It is only by becoming a servant that I submit in obedience to the King. In this submission the kingdom mindset is revealed in which God's good, pleasing and perfect will is shown in my life. Again, it comes with a price, for I have to be willing to die of self and lay down my ambitions and dreams of greatness and power! I have to let go of the Levitical model where I am the local priest maintaining and overseeing the local temple and programs. I have to become a servant to help the others serve as priests with kingdom authority.**

To do this work as servant, I need to look at the others through the eyes of Jesus and build them up to function as royal priests. But there is a very important thing to note: Not only do I have to look at them through the eyes of Jesus, but I have to also see myself through his eyes and I need his grace to do this. Thus the passage that follows the above, Romans 12:3-8, says: *For by the grace given me I say to every one of you: Do not think of yourself more highly than you ought, but rather think of yourself with sober judgment, in accordance with the measure of faith God has given you. Just as each of us has one body with many members and these members do not all have the same function, so in Christ we who are many form one body, and each member belongs to all the others. We have different gifts, according to the grace given us. If a man's gift is prophesying, let him use it in proportion to his faith. If it is serving, let him serve; if it is teaching, let him teach; if it is encouraging, let him encourage; if it is contributing to the needs of others, let him give generously; if it is leadership, let him govern diligently; if it is showing mercy, let him do it cheerfully.*

This is the point to note: I am nothing else than a member of the body, no more or less than anyone else. We are all royal priests in the order of Melchizedek. We have only one head, Jesus. He is the eternal High Priest and there is no hierarchy of priests and Levites to manage the body as his anointed representatives. This is why there are to be no titles indicating special positions, for we are all brothers in Christ, as Jesus himself said in Matthew 23 when he warned his disciples not to follow the practice of the Pharisees. We walk by faith and not by sight, but everything Pharisees did was done for men to see. Listen to Matthew 23:8-12: *But you are not to be called 'Rabbi,' for you have only one Master and you are all brothers. And do not call anyone on earth 'father,' for you have one Father and he is in heaven. Nor are you to be called 'teacher,' for you have one Teacher, the Christ. The greatest among you will be your servant. For whoever exalts himself will be humbled, and whoever humbles himself will be exalted.* It is not about titles! We often confuse function and title in our religious circles. Nowhere in the New Testament do we find any leader in the church addressed by a title. We read about apostles and it will be stated that someone like Paul is an apostle, but nowhere do we find anyone addressed as apostle or pastor or anything like that. In fact, the same is true in much of our society, e. g. Eda worked as secretary in a local school for many years. She was addressed as Mrs. Joubert, never secretary Joubert!

Let us begin to put the pieces together. Just above we saw that we have different gifts, according to the grace given to us, including leadership. As leaders we are to 'govern diligently.' This has been interpreted for the most part in terms of the worldly model and practiced as such in the church. However, let us look at it through the eyes of Jesus, our example. The first step in governing diligently is to humble ourselves and become servants. Further, diligent governing is nothing else than obedience to the task assigned to us, which is to equip and to enable each member to function as fully and as efficiently as possible in the body. Our task is to be servants encouraging the members to hear the voice of God and to walk in the Spirit. The best way to do this is to set an example by walking the walk ourselves. In the words of Paul to the church in Corinth, 1 Corinthians 10:31-11:1: *So whether you eat or drink or whatever you do, do it all for the glory of God. Do not cause anyone to stumble, whether Jews, Greeks or the church of God – even as I try to please everybody in every way. For I am not seeking my own good, but the good of many, so that they may be saved. Follow my example as I follow the example of Christ.*

We will return to this again in a moment, but let us take another look at Romans 12, this time verses 9-21 which spells out the walk of faith for which Paul set the example: *Love must be sincere. Hate what is evil; cling to what is good. Be devoted to one another in brotherly love. Honor one another above yourselves. Never be lacking in zeal, but keep your spiritual fervor, serving the Lord. Be joyful in hope, patient in affliction, faithful in prayer. Share with God's people who are in need. Practice hospitality. Bless those who persecute you; bless and do not curse. Rejoice with those who rejoice; mourn with those that mourn. Live in harmony with one another. Do not be proud, but be willing to associate with people of low position. Do not be conceited. Do not repay anyone evil for evil. Be careful to do what is right in the eyes of everybody. If it is possible, so far as it depends on you, live in peace with everybody. Do not take revenge, my friends, but leave room for God's wrath, for it is written: "It is mine to avenge; I will repay" says the Lord. On the contrary:*

"If your enemy is hungry, feed him;
if he is thirsty, give him something to drink.
In doing this, you will be heaping burning coals on his head."

Do not be overcome by evil, but overcome evil with good.

Leadership in the body is given in servant hood by being a catalyst for the other members to release them in their ministry. This is radically different than what happens in most churches, particularly when it comes to the issue of associating with people of low position. This is not just in terms of social position, but equally important in associating with those who are not considered to be spiritually mature or gifted. God seems to often choose the least likely people to accomplish what seems to be impossible. There are numerous examples from Scripture, as we know: Moses, who begged God to send someone else; Gideon, the 'mighty warrior' who was the least of the least likely family and hiding in the wine press; David, the youngest son who was not even considered by his father as possible chosen king and Paul who said of himself in 1 Corinthians 15:8-10 that *Christ appeared to him also, as one who was abnormally born, for "I am the least of the apostles and do not even deserve to be called an apostle, because I persecuted the church of God. But by the grace of God I am what I am, and his grace to me was not without effect. No, I worked harder than all of them – yet not I, but the grace of God that was in me."* **God can use anybody and he will often use the least likely person for the task, even if he has to use a donkey to speak to a prophet! As we moved out of the world of the church our eyes were opened by God's grace to begin to see the potential in 'the least.'** It also took a load off of our shoulders, for no longer do we need to make things happen. As we allowed the least to minister and encouraged them, the body grew and the level of faith increased. In the process we learned the truth that we need every member, especially those that we would never choose in our humanity and it is clearly mentioned in 1 Corinthians 12:18-27: *But in fact God has arranged the parts in the body, every one of them, just as he wanted them to be. If they were all one part, where would the body be?*

As it is, there are many parts, but one body. The eye cannot say to the hand, "I do not need you!" And the head cannot say to the feet, "I do not need you!" On the contrary, those parts of the body that seem to be weaker are indispensable, and the parts that we think are less honorable we treat with special honor. And the parts that are unpresentable we treat with special modesty, while our presentable parts do not need special treatment. But God has combined the members of the body and has given greater honor to the parts that lacked it, so that there should be no division in the body, but that its parts should have equal concern for each other. If one part suffers, every part suffers with it; if one part is honored, every part rejoices with it. Now you are the body of Christ and each one of you is part of it.

My task as a leader is to become a servant to the body by equipping the saints for their work of ministry and by encouraging them to function as a body. In the words of Romans 12:8, if I am called to leadership I am to govern diligently and this means I have to make sure that every member is equipped and released in ministry. This has nothing to do with running programs, for we are not called to be an organization, but we are the body of Christ. The leader is not to be served by the members, but must set the example as servant. This is precisely what Paul did as we read in 2 Corinthians6: 3-10: *We put no stumbling block in anyone's path, so that our ministry will not be discredited. Rather, as servants of God we commend ourselves in every way: in great endurance; in troubles, hardships and distresses; in beatings, imprisonments and riots; in hard work, sleepless nights and hunger; in purity, understanding, patience and kindness; in the Holy Spirit and in sincere love; in truthful speech and in the power of God; with weapons of righteousness in the right hand and in the left; through glory and dishonor, bad report and good report; genuine, yet regarded as impostors; known, yet regarded as unknown; dying, and yet we live on; beaten, and yet not killed; sorrowful, yet always rejoicing; poor, yet making many rich; having nothing, yet possessing everything.*

It is time to wrap this up, so let us return to the beginning of the chapter. In his grace God brought us to the point of moving out of the Levitical system and into the wilderness where we learned to seek him. In the wilderness, stripped of everything religious, we began to seek God in an intensely personal way. In the process we found many that were like sheep without a shepherd and needed a healing touch. However, in his grace God also forced us through circumstances and lack of resources to live and experience church as the body of Christ in a small group meeting with us in the home and at times just being there as a couple. We learned how to be the church and how to lead as described above. God graciously opened some doors to share the truths we learned with others and connected us with members of his body walking the walk in the wilderness. **Ultimately it is a choice of two styles of leadership. The Levitical system manifesting in religious leaders managing the programs opposed Jesus and ultimately rejected and nailed him to the cross. As followers of Jesus we chose to lay down our leadership with titles and positions of power to run an organization and make a name for ourselves. We chose to become servants in the order of Melchizedek as**

outlined in the letter to the Hebrews. With that choice we lost the financial base and security which allowed us to 'do ministry in the world of the church' and many simply avoided us. At the same time, it gave us an amazing freedom and we need to consider this freedom that comes when we trust God for our provision.

FREEDOM TO TRUST OUR FATHER FOR OUR PROVISION

It is interesting how specific events and words that greatly touch our lives at a given point in time, are used again by the Lord at another time to move us to a deeper knowledge and experience of faith. In a real sense the words that moved me to let go of my choice to become an engineer and moved me into "full time ministry"[7] spoke a new message under these circumstances, as I now read Matthew 8:18-22:

[7] At the time we understood "full time ministry" to mean becoming a pastor in the traditional sense of the word. Now we know ministry is full time for every member of the body, for all we do should be to honor our Lord.

When Jesus saw the crowd around him, he gave orders to cross to the other side of the lake. Then a teacher of the law came to him and said, "Teacher, I will follow you wherever you go."

Jesus replied: "Foxes have holes and the birds of the air have nests, but the Son of man has no place to lay his head."

Another disciple came to him and said: "Lord, first let me go and bury my father."

But Jesus told him: "Follow me and let the dead bury their own dead."

Following Jesus, our journey led us out of the security offered by the Levitical system. At first it did not look like freedom at all. As "pastor" in the Levitical system I had the perks and support that allowed me to 'do the work of ministry': I had the approved credentials needed for the position with a specific title that opened doors; I had the power to manage the programs, volunteers and staff and oversee the organization; I had a regular income and the perks of a vehicle, housing and medical coverage to meet the needs of my family and a pension plan for the future needs; and then the opportunity of working my way up through the ranks to gain more. **However, we walked away from these things and met Jesus in the wilderness. There the Scriptures came to life as we grasped what the order of Melchizedek meant. In the process we were set free to follow the example of Jesus and we were set free from the restrictions of the Levitical order and its legalism to walk in the**

Spirit. In time we were tested in the furnace and the heat was turned up considerably. Everything that gave us security was shaken and we were challenged more and more to walk in ways that defied any logic – facing increased pressure and at the same time ever diminishing support. Those that could help us chose not to do so for the most part and the Spirit clearly led us away from the worldly models of ministry support as practiced in North America and many other parts of the world.

To set the stage for this, let us turn to Jesus' words in Matthew 6:19-24: *Do not store up for yourselves treasures on earth, where moth and rust destroy, and where thieves break in and steal. But store up for yourselves treasures in heaven, where moth and rust do not destroy and thieves do not break in and steal. For where your treasure is, your heart will be also. The eye is the lamp of the body. If your eyes are good, your whole body will be full of light. But if your eyes are bad, your whole body will be full of darkness. If then the light within you is darkness, how great is that darkness. No one can serve two masters. Either he will hate the one and love the other, or he will be devoted to the one and despise the other. You cannot serve both God and money.*

Frankly we face a choice: We will work with a Levitical system with a focus on earthly temples with programs overseen by paid professional clergy or we will work in the order of Melchizedek where each member is a royal priest without earthly temples, programs and professionals. The first is seen by the buildings, advertised programs and leaders with robes and titles doing the work of ministry. It leads to a hierarchy of paid and non-paid modern priests and Levites and is run in a business-like way (sometimes poorly run, but nonetheless functioning like a business). Members are expected to support this through monetary gifts called tithes and offerings, which are often supplemented by special fund raisers like suppers and bake sales, even bingos. The order of Melchizedek in contrast does not depend on paid leaders, on special buildings that need to be maintained or on programs. It flows from a Kingdom vision that has a focus of investment in heaven, which means its earthly focus is on people as eternal resources. Instead of pouring resources into buildings, programs and professionals, those who understand their ministry in the order of Melchizedek pour their resources into people as they listen and respond to leading of the Spirit. We will return to this in the next chapter when we look at the freedom to handle Kingdom resources, but for now we need to turn our focus onto the source of our ministry resources, because **he who pays the piper calls the tune!**

Before we look at the words of Jesus about the source of our resources and support, it is vital to stress the key issue again: The Old Testament Levitical system was totally abolished in Christ and replaced by the order of Melchizedek. In the letter to the Hebrews this is the theme throughout and summed up in Hebrews 8:13: *By calling this covenant "new," he has made the first one obsolete;*

and what is obsolete and aging will soon disappear. In Christ Jesus the old system, based on an earthly High Priest supported by a caste of priests and Levites to do the ministry, was replaced by the order of Melchizedek where Jesus is the eternal and only High Priest and all members of the body become royal priests. **With this the need to have a special caste of priests to run programs, maintain special buildings and do ministry on behalf of the people and for the people became obsolete.** Leaders were simply to be servants. They worked as itinerant leaders supporting themselves in secular jobs and occasionally receiving voluntary gifts as the members of the body were led to give, as we know from the life of Paul. This did not mean that leaders could not expect support for their work, as Paul himself explained in 1 Corinthians 9, **but this support was never as settled 'pastors' in a local church receiving a salary (by whatever other name) with housing and other perks, to do the work of ministry as we have today!** In fact, the church functioned for centuries. without special buildings, programs and pastors in our modern way. The change was solidified when Constantine as emperor converted to Christianity and enforced the change in the structure of the church to come in line with the Roman Empire's structure, so that the 'spiritual structure' mirrored the political structure.[8] In this way the order of Melchizedek was abolished and a Christianized Levitical system was implemented,

[8] James Rutz gives a great summary of the history leading to this in Appendix 2 of the book "Mega Shift."

formulated to be like the worldly Roman Empire in spiritual clothing. What had been declared to have been made obsolete by Christ was now revived again and with that money and the control thereof became central in the church. Instead of a living organism the church for the most part became an institution run by professionals. Thus programs and ways to obtain resources for the maintenance of the institution and its managers began to play a major role in the church.

This also brought about the ungodly division of the body into clergy and laity. With this division there also came the power struggles between the two groups which has continued for centuries and will continue as long as this division exists. The clergy became dependent on the laity as source of their supply, however spiritual it may be presented. They had to invent ways to get and keep getting the supply through 'stewardship teaching' and other ways of manipulation. As a result, many abuses were brought into the church, from the indulgences of the Middle ages to the misuse of sacraments and the exclusion of laity from the Lord's table and in some circles from preaching and teaching. It also led to the 'teachings on giving' necessary to support the institution. The flip side of this has been the manipulation and control and abuse of clergy by controllers in the church. As we stated above, he who pays the piper calls the tune! If some do not like the 'manager,' he or she is expendable and can be replaced. All of these are the results of the worldly structure imposed upon the church. **In this process**

the simplicity of the New Testament teaching on resources is totally missed, especially the freedom to handle these to first meet the needs of the needy and the freedom to support the work of ministry as led by the Spirit. Moreover, money becomes such a powerful idol that most, even sincere believers, do not understand that the real source of all our resources is God. Let us look at the passage following Jesus' teaching on storing treasures in heaven, Matthew 6:25-34.

Therefore, I tell you, do not worry about your life, what you will eat or drink; or about your body, what you will wear. Is not life more important than food, and the body more than clothes? Look at the birds of the air; they do not sow or reap or store away in barns, and yet your heavenly Father feeds them. Are you not more valuable than they? Who of you by worrying can add a single hour to your life?

And why do you worry about clothes? See how the lilies of the field grow. They do not labor or spin. Yet I tell you that not even Solomon in all his splendor was dressed like one of these. If that is how God clothes the grass of the field, which is here today and tomorrow is thrown into the fire, will he not much more clothe you, O you of little faith? So do not worry, saying, "What shall we eat?" or "What shall we drink?" or "What shall we wear?" For the pagans run after all these things, and your heavenly Father knows that you need them. But seek first his kingdom and his righteousness, and all these things will be given to you as well. Therefore do not worry about tomorrow, for tomorrow will worry about itself. Each day has enough trouble of its own.

Now these words when taken at face value have some major implications for our 'Christian community' and for the way we handle our resources. Take for example the whole industry handling investments by Christians and those working in the area of insurance, for both of these are the direct result of worrying about the future and in the words of Jesus it is the way of the pagans! **Jesus' solution for the planning of the future is to seek first the Kingdom and its righteousness and trust that God will take care of the worldly needs. This is far too radical for most of us, so we will make these words into a little chorus and sing it as part of the Levitical Sunday program and then put something in an envelope to cover the religious segment of our lives. Then we walk out into the world and trust our employer to meet our needs while seeking the advice of the investment industry guru to plan for the future. After all, what if we seek Jesus' Kingdom and he challenges us like he challenged he rich young ruler? Or what if we seek his Kingdom and the Spirit directs us to give to someone in need that which we have set aside for 'our tithe' or for our retirement investments?** It is risky business and not prudent to take Jesus too seriously! Again, we will look at these issues in the next chapter when we deal with the freedom to handle resources, but let us keep the focus on the issue of leadership in the church and trusting God for provision.

The current Levitical system practiced by the institutional churches is led and overseen by salaried employees known as clergy who are hired to do the ministry. The preferred titles are priests, ministers and pastors. Regardless of the title, their work is seen as "pastoring the flock." It is significant that the word 'pastor,' referring to leadership in a way remotely related to the idea of accepted church leadership, is only found in one passage of the New Testament. The other references to pastor or pastoring refer exclusively to Jesus Christ as the Shepherd, except two passages where the task is expressly assigned to the elders (plural). However we want to define 'elder,' it was not a term referring to professionals, but to mature leaders in the local communities and interchangeable with the term bishop (overseer), likewise not a reference to a professional spiritual leader. With that said, it is good to read the one passage where we do find the reference to pastor as leader grouped with other leaders and defining the work of 'the pastor,' Ephesians 4:11: *"It was he (Christ) who gave some to be apostles, some to be prophets, some to be evangelists, and some to be pastors and teachers, to prepare God's people for works of service, so that the body of Christ may be built up until we all reach unity in the faith and in the knowledge of the Son of God and become mature, attaining to the whole measure of the fullness of Christ.* Now, regardless of how one interprets these leadership terms (and some simply group them under one 'office' called pastor or priest or minister,) **they have only one task and that is to equip the members for the work of ministry!** A simple application of this to the church would imply that the task of the pastor or leader is done as soon as the members have learned to look after one another! In fact, this is exactly what Paul did as we follow his ministry. He never settled in one church for long and when he left or was forced to leave, the people were functioning without an appointed pastor to do the work of ministry. He equipped and released them to do the work and moved on. **The mark of Biblical leadership is seen in people equipped and released to function as the body of the Lord and doing the work of ministry as royal priests. This means that, if we were to look at the church as a business venture (as practiced in the Institutional Church), then we need to immediately fire every pastor settled in a church for a number of years if the people are not able to function without him or her. Further, if they are, then the work is done and 'the pastor' is to move on and there should be no need to have another one come to fill the vacant spot! This is simply applying sound management standards to the worldly model practiced in the Institutional Church. If someone is not doing his job effectively, he should be fired.**

As it is, this will not happen in most churches and few will even consider this if challenged, **because most people and leaders in the church have never even recognized the fact that they are through tradition bound to the Levitical structure that**

Jesus Christ abolished. For most in the western world being a believer is linked to being a member of the institutional church in one form or another. As we have seen, leadership has been changed (and is unchallenged as concept) to be understood as a Christianized Levitical priest who is hired to do the ministry and to represent the people before God and God before the people. In a word, in the world of the church the 'pastor' is hired to be a mediator and is therefore usurping the place of Christ who is our only mediator.

Being hired by the local church as minister effectively makes the pastor depend on the people's giving as source of supply for his or her work. In fact, when I was ordained one of the key clauses in the call included a statement as to the projected income of the church and that the agreed portion for my salary was to be **the first priority of the church.** Having a group of people pay one's salary makes one particularly vulnerable to the perceived needs and expectations of the people and one often faces the pressures of opposing expectations which lead to no-win situations. Running afoul of a key controlling personality often means being ousted from the ministry. Further, when power plays happen, overseeing church authorities will usually choose against the pastor, for it is easier to sacrifice one person than to deal with resolving the issues, not unlike the advice of Caiaphas, the Levitical High Priest, to the Jews regarding Jesus as recorded in John 18:14. One has to be adept at power politics to survive in ministry as practiced in many churches and denominations and those who relish power plays often rise to the top of the pyramid. The flip side of the coin is that the Levitical system empowers the leaders in unhealthy ways and this opens the door to the exploitation and abuse of vulnerable members by clergy, as illustrated in recent years by revelations and lawsuits on behalf of victims.

We can expand the list in more ways, but let us return to other implications of the pastor being dependent on the people's giving as source of supply. The Levitical system is inherently costly and consumes resources in wasteful ways when compared to the order of Melchizedek. The cost of running the institutional church adds pressure to the pastor. For one, the pastor needs to be gifted in many ways to attract enough members and to encourage these members to give adequately to cover the costs related to the organization. This is no easy task in our consumer society where people shop for their 'spiritual needs' in the same way they do for products. Add to that the fact that the Levitical system, birthed in the division of the body into clergy and laity, inevitably gave rise to denominational and other divisions competing for their share of Christian consumers in the religious marketplace and the task of the local pastor becomes very daunting indeed. It is not easy to maintain and grow the organization in the midst of the religious market with so many competing within the body at large for a share of the faithful and with pressures of other religions and the secularism of modern society drawing people away. Those in smaller churches face tremendous pressures and, like the corporate world, the bigger church conglomerates swallow the little churches and doors close – and many pastors suffer as a result. The expectations placed on those in ministry are so enormous that it is no surprise that many burn out or leave the ministry altogether. Those that stay learn to live and manage the world of the church and learn to compromise the truth they know, because of their dependence on the income from the local church. They often move from church to church while little is accomplished and someone else takes your place and the cycle is repeated. 'Churches' live and die in the process and doors open and close. **However, within the Levitical system as practiced, there is a comfort zone for many as they grow up with it. The predictability of the rituals (even among many who consider themselves open to the Spirit) and the functions within the organization which reward individuals giving them a feeling of being needed, feed the religious needs in many. However, the bottom line is that the pastor's first priority is to concentrate on building and maintaining the local church. The result is that both the pastor and the members usually equate the local church with the Kingdom of God. This means that Jesus' words 'to first seek the Kingdom and its righteousness' are interpreted as 'building and maintaining the local church and its programs.'**

So, in the western church world our spiritual energy and resources are invested in 'our church.' The local church budget tells the story, as nothing else will, for by the fruit we recognize the tree. Time, energy, talent and resources are all poured into the local church and to encourage this even more we are by law allowed to hand out tax receipts. It sounds and looks good, until we turn the light of Scripture to these matters! For starters, the whole underlying Levitical structure becomes very obvious when we look at the stewardship teachings to encourage giving in support of the church. **At the heart of the teaching, we find the stress on giving tithes to the local church (equivalent of the Old Covenant's temple) with the key needs to maintain the buildings and programs and to pay the salaries of the professional clergy (the modern equivalent of the Old Covenant's priests and Levites).** Offerings are considered to be over and above tithes (at least in some evangelical circles) and these cover things like special donations for needy, itinerant preachers, missions, 'para-church ministries, etc. **So, we first give to ourselves and the leftovers are for the 'wider needs in the body.' In fact, if you are invited to a church as a guest speaker or as itinerant worker have special meetings, it is very important when taking an offering to stress that those in attendance give an offering and that their tithe belongs to the local church! After all, invitations to speak in local churches open the door for income to itinerant ministers and one**

cannot afford to alienate the leaders who open these doors.

The problem with this is that we do not find any of this in the New Testament and among the teaching of the apostles! In fact, as we have noticed earlier, they had no church buildings that needed to be maintained, no settled clergy serving as priests and no programs that needed resources. **The resources were used for most part to meet the real needs of people, particularly the poor, orphans and widows. In addition to this, itinerant leaders were occasionally blessed and their work supported by individuals and churches and hospitality was widely practiced. When needed secular employment provided leaders with income to meet needs as they traveled. In this they trusted God to provide while they obeyed the Spirit as they moved and ministered, learning to be content whatever the circumstances.**

This is the issue: If we do not depend 100% on the Father for our provision, we will struggle to become faithful stewards. Unless we realize that all we have is from the Father, a gift from heaven, we will not invest it all in the Kingdom. This is true for every single person on earth, but especially important for those who are called to be leaders in the church. The dependence of leaders on the financial support through the church means that they are confined by the institutional ties in ministry and would for example never have been able to respond to a vision and immediately cross the seas as Paul and his companions did when he saw the Macedonian man - recorded in Acts 16:9-10. In fact, one of the main reasons we do not relate to the church in the book of Acts is that the freedom of the Spirit is so foreign to our worldly church culture. Our churches demand leaders that are managers of the status quo, receiving their marching orders from those who pay their salaries and who want to be served without discomfort. To fully depend on the Father for provision and to listen to the voice of the Spirit who is as unpredictable as the wind, is not possible in the four walls and the safe comfort of the church zone with its programs and services. However, it is not easy to step out of this safe comfort and learn to walk in faith for daily provision. It is especially difficult in our church culture that has been so skewed by the Levitical mentality, as it is so wasteful when it comes to resources. The best way to describe this is to look to the story of the Canaanite woman recorded in Matthew 15:21-28. The story opens with this heathen woman seeking Jesus to heal her demon possessed daughter. Jesus continued to ignore her pleas, but she would not give up and it frustrated the disciples who urged him to send her away. Then we read:

Jesus answered: "I was sent only to the lost sheep of Israel."

The woman came and knelt before him. "Lord, help me!" she said.

He replied: "<u>It is not right to take the children's bread and toss it to their dogs.</u>"

"Yes, Lord," she said, but even the dogs eat the crumbs that fall from their masters' table."

Then Jesus answered, "Woman, you have great faith. Your request is granted." And her daughter was healed from that very hour.

In a similar way those who dare to walk out of the world of the church today will find that unless they aggressively battle for a share of the resources in the hands of believers, they will only get the occasional crumb from the table. The Levitical leaders and institutions, that have a vested interest in the status quo, control the bread and there is powerful opposition to anything that may be viewed as competition for the religious slice of the world market. In fact, when we personally heeded the voice of the Spirit and walked through the gates of control, we quickly became aware that we were in the wilderness. It was not easy to learn to trust God for provision and in our case, God used us as prophetic signs to many that knew us. In fact, many who knew us and serve the Lord could no longer fit us into their comfort zone and like the disciples in the story above would rather have had us disappear from view, than deal with the problem (and embarrassment) we presented. When we did not just disappear, they simply began to ignore us and pretended we did not exist. Others, especially those with many resources gave crumbs from the laden tables and even occasionally a piece of bread, but when we did not submit to the conventional wisdom to build 'a required support network,' but waited on the Lord and did what the Spirit directed, they withheld what they might have given. Some agonized about our situation, but did nothing. At first God had us working in secular jobs – and then directed Eda to stop. At the time my part-time income from the job disappeared as the company needed investment funds that were not to be found and God directed me to stay and pray with them without income. In the process we became very aware of the needs in the world and the lack of response from the church community, where the focus is not on people, but on building and maintaining the institution.

However, the other side of this coin is that we learned to walk in faith in ways we never understood before. We began to look at life through Kingdom eyes and we found that there were a few who truly knew the man Jesus and the Father. We found that those who have the fewest resources were often the ones who understood generosity and sacrifice. It was not easy, but with God's grace we began to understand and were able to relate to Paul's words in Philippians 4:10-13 when he thanked them for a gift he had received in these words:

I rejoice greatly in the Lord that at last you have renewed your concern for me. Indeed, you have been concerned, but you had no opportunity to show it. I am not saying this because I am in need, for I have learned to be content whatever the circumstances. I know what it is to be in need, and I know what it is to have plenty. I have learned the secret of being content in any and every situation, whether well fed or hungry, whether living in plenty or in want. I can do everything through him who gives me the strength.

It is not easy for most of us to live our lives conscious of our utter dependence on the Father's supply. Those who are called to full-time itinerant ministry like the apostles and apostolic team members in the five-fold ministry[9] face a very difficult task in today's western culture. It is not that there is a lack of resources for this work (there is ample!), but the mindsets of believers blinded by centuries of Levitical structures continue to divert the Kingdom resources into that which bear little or no fruit, but being blinded they do not see this. The result is that the most productive workers in the Kingdom of God often minister with little or no support, even to the point of being held back by the lack of support. **The fact is that those called to full-time itinerant ministry in the order of Melchizedek in our society face the realities mentioned above. Like the apostle Paul we better learn to be content whatever the situation. Having walked out of the world of the church with this call, I can testify to this. At this point it is important to**

[9] For those unfamiliar with this term, it refers to the five offices mentioned in Eph. 4:12, "Apostles, Prophets, Evangelists, Pastors and Teachers. A side note to this is that all five of these are itinerant ministries including that of pastor. Their task again is simply to equip the saints for their work of ministry and the task of the pastor is to equip the members to truly care for one another and thus not to become the settled resident pastor doing the pastoring!

take another look at the price Paul paid as he walked as apostle, e. g. 1 Corinthians 4:1,9-13:

So then, men ought to regard us as servants of Christ and as those entrusted with the secret things of God.

For it seems to me that God has put us apostles on display at the end of the procession, like men condemned to die in the arena. We have been made a spectacle to the whole universe, to angels as well as to men. We are fools for Christ, but you are so wise in Christ! We are weak, but you are strong! You are honored, we are dishonored! To this very hour we go hungry and thirsty, we are in rags, we are brutally treated, we are homeless. We work with our own hands. When we are cursed, we bless; when we are persecuted, we endure it; when we are slandered, we answer kindly. Up to this moment we have become the scum of the earth, the refuse of the world.

Listen, when the pressure comes, so will the temptation to walk away from it or to find a way out. When Jesus was filled with the Spirit at his baptism, the very next step was to be led into the wilderness where he was tempted. The first temptation came when he got hungry and the tempter suggested that he use his power to turn stones into bread. Many, who walk out of the world of the church and away from the comfort zone of a regular pay cheque, under pressure quickly succumb to the temptation to 'build a ministry with supporters' and have 'a resource table' to provide income and seek speaking engagements 'where they can take a love offering.' In fact, these things are spiritualized to become 'God's ways to provide.' **The**

temptation to return to the Levitical system and manipulate others to supply the provision is strong, when one faces the realities of hunger and thirst and basic needs. Worldly reasoning with selected Scriptures can quickly provide logical arguments to engage in raising one's support for the work of ministry.

It is important to note that it is not wrong to expect support for working in ministry. This is precisely what Paul addressed further in 1 Corinthians 9:1-14: *Am I not free? Am I not an apostle? Have I not seen Jesus our Lord? Are you not the result of my work in the Lord? Even though I may not be an apostle to others, surely I am one to you! For you are the seal of my apostleship in the Lord.*

This is my defense to those who sit in judgment of me. Don't we have the right to food and drink? Don't we have the right to take a believing wife along with us, as do the other apostles and the Lord's brothers and Cephas? Or is it only Barnabas and I who must work for a living?

Who serves as a soldier at his own expense? Who plants a vineyard and does not eat of its grapes? Who tends a flock and does not drink its milk? Do I say this merely from a human point of view? Doesn't the law say the same thing? For it is written in the law of Moses: "Do not muscle an ox while it is treading out the grain." Is it about oxen that God is concerned? Surely he says this for us, doesn't he? Yes, this was written for us, because when the plowman plows and the thresher threshes, they ought to do so in the hope of sharing in the harvest. If we have sown spiritual seed among you, is it too much if we reap a material harvest from you? If others have this right of support from you, shouldn't we have it all the more?

But we did not use this right. On the contrary, we put up with anything rather than hinder the gospel of Christ. Don't you know that those who work in the temple get their food from the temple, and those who serve at the altar share in what is offered on the altar. In the same way the Lord has commanded that those who preach the gospel should receive their living from the gospel. But I have not used any of these rights!

The issue is not whether someone in itinerant ministry can expect support as they do ministry. The issue is how this support is generated and received. First, we note yet again that the apostolic leaders in the early church did not serve as settled pastors receiving a salary from the local church. They were itinerant and served as the Spirit led them, traveling in teams and often accompanied by their wives. However, their support was voluntary as the Spirit led the believers. Thus leaders would serve as Paul did in Corinth without any remuneration for his ministry and on other occasions receive specific gifts from other churches or individuals. Occasionally they did other work, e. g. Paul chose not to exercise the right of expecting support and thus worked as tent maker at times. In fact, Paul addressed this at length in 2 Corinthians 10-11. The key difference between him and

the false apostles was seen in the fact that he was willing to pay the price to minister freely, whereas the false apostles took advantage of the people and exploited them as we read in 2 Corinthians 11:20.

This brings us right back to where we started in the chapter. We have to choose whether or not we will follow Jesus who had no place to call his own, as he said in Matthew 8:20! We have to choose whether we will trust the Father to provide for our needs, or whether we want to manipulate the people and use the ministry to bring provision. **The real question is where we find our security.** We will either serve Mammon (and all it can provide – housing, food, clothing, income, pensions, benefits and investments) or we will serve God. We will either use the worldly system (in its religious clothing) to get provision as most ministries and churches do, or we will trust God and live in faith, trusting the Father for provision. **We will either seek the Kingdom of God and his righteousness, or we will build and seek to maintain our own earthly kingdom using religious manipulation to get resources for our plans.**

Who or what we see as the source of our provision will determine how we handle the resources at our disposal. However, before we move to that, it is important to address the issue of supplementary income through 'secular work' to enable a leader to do 'ministry.' In a word, we have found that many who are called to itinerant ministry choose to secure a full or part time job for provision, particularly due to the fact that the worldly church culture has such a strong hold over the resources in the hands of believers that itinerant ministers often suffer. Thus, one is forced to join the prevailing world of the church and its methods of marketing one's ministry contrary to Scripture or one has to find another source of income through secular employment. In this the history of Paul who occasionally worked as tent maker is used as example to support the decision to work in a secular field. **In itself there is nothing wrong with that, provided that the Spirit leads one to do this! However, in many ways it has become yet another way of seeking one's support from the world instead of trusting the Father. Paul's particular job allowed him freedom to travel and minister without being tied to a local area. In addition, he did not do this all the time, but trusted the Lord and learned to be content as we have seen. The key is to listen to the Spirit and follow him no matter what people say or think – even when it makes no sense at all. However, until we walk in faith in full dependence upon our Father for provision, we will not listen to the Spirit with an openness to follow him wherever he may lead us.**

With that it is time to move to the next key issue and that is the freedom to give. In this regard it is very enlightening to read a portion of Jesus' instructions to the first itinerant ministers he sent out as recorded in Matthew 10:7-16, for it speaks of the faith for provision: *As you go, preach this message: "The Kingdom of heaven is near." Heal the sick, raise the dead, cleanse those who have leprosy, drive out demons. Freely you have received, freely give. Do not take along any gold or silver or copper in your belts; take no bag for the journey, or extra tunic, or sandals or a staff; for the worker is worth his keep. Whatever town or village you enter, search for some worthy person there and stay at his house until you leave. As you enter the house, give it your greeting. If the home is deserving, let your peace rest on it; if it is not, let your peace return to you. If anyone will not welcome you or listen to your words, shake the dust off your feet when you leave that home or town. I tell you the truth, it will be more bearable for Sodom and Gomorrah on the day of judgment than for that town. I am sending you like sheep among wolves. Therefore, be as shrewd as snakes and as innocent as doves.*

The freedom to give flows directly from the freedom to receive. Until we know how to trust the Father for our provision in every way, we will not be able to freely handle the Kingdom resources available to us in righteousness. As long as we trust our worldly wisdom dressed in religious clothing to bring provision, we will continue to misuse the resources we have. In the process we will continue to miss the very presence of God as he steps into our world in the person in need, just as Israel missed the presence of God in Jesus and as Jerusalem missed the very visitation of God on the day he entered the city on the back of a little donkey. Like the Pharisees and teachers of the law most of us are so blinded by our religious buildings and programs with the paid speakers doing the work of ministry, that we miss the presence of our Lord when he shows up and overturns our theology. We tithe and give offerings to spend it on our buildings and programs while the poor and needy go hungry.[10] We give a portion of 'what we earned' to the religious institution for a tax receipt and walk by the hurting, trusting the government welfare to look after them. Like the Pharisees we diligently teach the principles of 'tithing and giving and stewardship' (to serve the needs of the Levitical system), but we neglect the more important matters of the law – justice, mercy and faithfulness. **However, those who learn to trust the Father fully for all their needs are set free to become Kingdom givers. They are able to handle the resources with a freedom that defies logic. They walk through life with a divine discernment and recognize Jesus in situations where the priests and Levites pass by. What they have is multiplied by the divine power of the Father who owns the cattle on a thousand hills. They are able to give everything away – even their livelihood, knowing the gold and silver all belongs to the Father and they have access to a storehouse that will never be empty. Let us now look at this freedom which is not found in the four walls of any institution by any name!**

[10] In our religious (and secular) culture there is a great stress on and desire to operate with "charitable status." In most cases it is simply a way to operate a business by abusing the system set up to do charitable work in order to avoid taxes. Thus we have many 'Charities," but little if any charity!

THE FREEDOM TO HANDLE RESOURCES WITH KINGDOM MINDED RIGHTEOUSNESS

It is interesting to look at Matthew 6 again. In verse 33 Jesus said that when we first seek the Kingdom of God and his righteousness, all our needs would be met. If we go back to the beginning of the chapter, we read the following: *Be careful not to do your acts of righteousness before men, to be seen by them. If you do you will have no reward from your Father in heaven. So when you give to the needy, do not announce it with trumpets, as the hypocrites do in the synagogues and on the streets, to be honored by men. I tell you the truth, they have received their reward in full. But when you give to the needy, do not let your left hand know what your right hand is doing, so that your giving may be in secret. Then your Father, who sees what is done in secret, will reward you.*

No matter how we want to slice this, central to the righteousness that flows from Kingdom living is the care of those in need. In fact, a simple reading of the New Testament will reveal that the resources of the early church were almost exclusively given to support the needs of the poor, orphans and widows. In addition, support gifts were occasionally given to itinerant leaders in the church. **We find that they did not spend money on anything else than the above mentioned. Please note that not one penny was recorded as having been spent on buildings (whether construction of a church or maintenance) – although some want to read into Acts 19:9-10 that Paul rented the hall. We do not know if he did and there is no evidence that he took any offerings to cover the costs. My guess is that if rent were required Paul would likely have paid it out of his own pocket. The only collections he took were for the care of the poor. Nothing was spent on programs or on resident clergy's salaries and needs. Not one penny was spent on maintaining a head office and denominational staff overseeing and developing programs. The resources were available to meet the real needs of real people, for the believers trusted the Father for provision and responded as the Spirit would lead, to care for the church that they knew was not an institution, but the people themselves.**

Before we look at this in more detail, let us see for ourselves how they lived and handled the resources entrusted to them by the Father. As we read this, keep in mind that they had far fewer resources than what we have in our western world today. This is the story in the words of Luke in Acts 2:42-47: *They devoted themselves to the apostles' teaching and to the fellowship, to the breaking of bread and to prayer. Everyone was filled with awe and many miraculous signs and wonders were done by the apostles. All the believers were together and had everything in common. Selling their possessions and goods, they gave to anyone as he had needs. Every day they continued to meet together in the temple courts. They broke bread in their homes and ate together with glad and sincere hearts, praising God and enjoying the favor of all the people. And the Lord added to their number daily those who were being saved.*

This is again mentioned with more detail in Acts 4:32-37 which reads as follows: *All the believers were one in heart and mind. No one claimed that any of his possessions was his own, but they shared everything they had. With great power the apostles continued to testify to the resurrection of the Lord Jesus and much grace was upon them all. There were no needy persons among them. For from time to time those who owned lands or houses sold them, brought the money from the sales and put it at the apostles' feet, and it was distributed to anyone as he had need. Joseph, a Levite from Cyprus, whom the apostles called Barnabas (which means son of encouragement), sold a field he owned and brought the money and put it at the apostles' feet.*

Now, how many of our churches can say that there is no one in the church with needs that are not met? How many of us can truly say that the local church in town is growing and has the favor of all the people? How common is it to hear that some sold possessions and goods to meet the need of another? If someone were to sell his house or property and give it to a local leader, how likely is it that the money will be spent in its entirety to meet the needs of the less privileged? How many will trust local leaders enough to simply hand money from a sale of property to them with no questions asked and fully believing it will not be misused or applied to things like buildings, salaries and programs?

So how did they manage to live like this? What is the key to such generosity and trust? **The answer is in the passage above: They were in unity, for they understood that the church is nothing other than the believers as the body of the risen Lord. They were tied together under one head, Jesus Christ, and every single one was a member of the body. Jesus was their Lord and King and they became servants of the Kingdom. As such they were entrusted with Kingdom resources given by the Father who has access to inexhaustible storehouses. They understood these things and thus no one claimed that his possessions were his own. All they had were for the sake of the Kingdom and they had a never-ending supply, for they knew the source of the resources, the Father. Thus they could be overflowing in generosity!**

Let us take a look at Acts 4:32 again and note that *"no one claimed that his possessions were his own."* Most of us have never really grasped that all we have is a simple gift from the Father. In this regard it is important to read Paul's words in 1 Timothy 6:6-10: *But godliness with contentment is great gain. For we brought nothing into the world and we can take nothing out of it. But if we have food and clothing, we will be content with that. People who want to get rich fall into temptation and a trap, and into many foolish and harmful desires that plunge men into ruin and destruction. For the love of money is a root of all kinds of evil. Some people, eager for money, have wandered from the faith and pierced themselves with many griefs.*

Let us focus on the fact that we did not bring anything into this world and will not take anything out of it. As someone said: "You never see a hearse pull a U-Haul!" In fact, no single one of us even chose to be born. We did not consult our parents and they did not consult us! Our very existence and lives are gifts from God. In the words of Isaiah 40:6 *all men are like grass and their glory is like the flowers of the field. The grass withers and the flowers fall, because the breath of the Lord blows on them. Surely the people are grass. The grass withers and the flowers fall, but the word of our God stands forever.* These words speak for themselves. They speak even louder when we read the words of Jesus in Luke 12:13-21: *Someone in the crowd said to him: "Teacher, tell my brother to divide the inheritance with me."*

Jesus replied: "Man, who appointed me a judge or an arbiter between you?" Then he said to them: "Watch out! Be on your guard against all kinds of greed; a man's life does not consist in the abundance of his possessions."

And he told them this parable: "The ground of a certain rich man produced a good crop. He thought to himself, 'what shall I do? I have no place to store my crops.' Then he said: 'This is what I'll do. I will tear down my barns and build bigger ones, and there I will store all my grain and my goods. And I will say to myself, "You have plenty of good things laid up for many years. Take life easy; eat, drink and be merry."'

But God said to him: 'You fool. This very night your life will be demanded from you. Then who will get what you have prepared for yourself?'

This then is how it will be with anyone who stores up things for himself but is not rich toward God.

Jesus' words fly in the face of most of our society's ideas including the very teaching given by our "Christian investment specialists" and those who are considered wise in the area of finances. It is precisely because we do not understand these things, that the teaching in the area of stewardship in the church misses the mark for the most part. Having been blinded by the accepted Levitical model of leadership, the focus has been on the church as institution with its needs and we miss the heartbeat of the Lord when it comes to the real needs of people. This is why we can walk by the hurting like the Levite and the priest in the parable of the good Samaritan, for we are made to feel good as long as we put a donation on the offering plate when we attend the church! We trust that the government's social programs and the church's benevolence fund, which is the crumb from the institutional table, will meet the needs. With the focus on the church (and ministries) as institution run by a Levitical hierarchy like the Old

Testament temple service, the key teaching is on tithes and offerings and how to run successful fund-raising campaigns. In addition to these we spend countless hours and resources to run bazaars, bake sales, church suppers and even 'Christian lotteries' like bingos and raffles. Those who really understand the concept, add the book and resource tables with tapes, T-shirts and whatever else to make money, all in the name of the Kingdom. When all is said and done, the majority of the funds are spent on maintaining the institutional needs of the church or ministry. All of this is done in the name of the Lord who overturned the tables of the money changers in the temple!

It is important to note that the story of Jesus' actions in the temple is found in every one of the four gospels. Without belaboring the point here, Jesus' actions were very pointedly focused on the misuse of authority to obtain funds from the public, as we read in Matthew 21:12-14: *Jesus entered the temple area and drove out all who were buying and selling there. He overturned the tables of the money changers and the benches of those selling doves. "It is written," he said to them, "My house will be called a house of prayer, but you are making it a den of robbers."* However we want to interpret his words and actions in the passage, the temple authorities were greatly angered and ultimately made sure that he was crucified. It is further important to see the rest of the story as recorded in Matthew 21, for it speaks to the whole matter in a powerful way.

Directly following the cleansing of the temple, a door to ministry opened bringing joy and freedom to many, for we read the following in Matthew 21:14-17: *The blind and the lame came to him at the temple, and he healed them. But when the chief priests and the teachers of the law saw the wonderful things he did and the children shouting in the temple area, "Hosanna to the son of David," they were indignant. "Do you hear what these children are saying?" they asked him. Jesus replied, "Yes, have you never read, 'From the lips of children and infants you have ordained praise'?" And he left them and went out of the city to Bethany where he spent the night.* **We need to note that the ministry to the lame and the blind took place without an ordained priest and did not require nor received the blessing and oversight of the religious hierarchy. This ministry also did not require or receive any funds that were being raised in the temple 'for the work of the Lord!' As Jesus ministered freely, joy erupted with children shouting forth his praise to the dismay and indignation of the religious leaders. In response to their question about the children, Jesus quoted from Psalm 8:2 – and it is significant that the rest of this verse speaks of the enemies of the Lord and that the children's praise silences the foe and avenger! The very day that the Lord stepped into the temple, the religious leadership opposed him and even though the fruit of his ministry was visible even to the children, the leaders missed the very presence of God. They were more concerned about the institution and**

their positions of authority in it, than about the presence of God.

It does not end here, though. The next passage in Matthew records the story of the unfruitful fig tree and how Jesus rebuked it and it withered immediately. This astonished the disciples and Jesus taught them about the power of faith and the prayer of faith. This story provides the setting of the next passages and it raises the question about the fruit or lack of fruit in ministry. The fruit of our ministry is directly related to our faith in Jesus and our submission to his authority. In Christ the Levitical order was replaced with the order of Melchizedek. The latter bore Kingdom fruit, but it also challenged the authority of Levitical leadership, as we read in the story that follows in Matthew 21:23-27: *Jesus entered the temple courts and while he was teaching, the chief priests and elders of the people came to him and asked: "By what authority are you doing these things and who gave you this authority?" Jesus replied: "I will also ask you one question. If you answer me, I will tell you by what authority I am doing these things. John's baptism – where did it come from? Was it from heaven or from men?" They discussed it among themselves and said, "If we say, 'from heaven,' he will ask, 'then why didn't you believe him?' But is we say, 'from men,' - we are afraid of the people, for they all hold that John was a prophet." So they answered Jesus, "We don't know." Then he said: "Neither do I tell you by what authority I am doing these things."*

Religion seeks submission to human authority in the persons of religious leaders representing

the institution. Religious spirits exercise control over people through rules, regulations and traditions set up by such religious leaders who have a vested interest in the institution that places resources at their control and provides their income. Therefore religious leaders and their followers fear the freedom of the Spirit and they fear those who walk in the freedom of the Spirit like Jesus did. The reason for this fear is that they find security in their ability to control people and resources. The Levitical leaders could not do this with Jesus. He ministered with authority – but they did not and could not control him. He presented a challenge to the Levitical authority and control then and he does so to this day. In Jesus Christ the order of Levi represented by the Levitical hierarchy under the Levitical high priest faced the order of Melchizedek with an eternal High Priest who walked in the freedom of the Spirit with divine authority. Rather than recognize him, they chose to oppose him, for in him their control over people and resources had to be relinquished. The same holds true today as we will shortly see. First, we have to look at the next stories recorded in Matthew 21, because they shed more light on the issue of control over resources.

Matthew 21:28-32 is the story of a father and two sons: *(Jesus said:) "What do you think? There was a man who had two sons. He went to the fist and said: 'Son, go and work today in the vineyard.' 'I will not,' he answered, but later he changed his mind and went. Then the father went to the other son and said the same thing. He answered, 'I will, sir,' but he did not go. Which of the two did what the father wanted?" "The first," they answered. Jesus said to them: "I tell you the truth, the tax collectors and the prostitutes are entering the kingdom of God ahead of you. For John came to show you the way of righteousness and you did not believe him, but the tax collectors and the prostitutes did. And even after you saw this, you did not repent and believe him."*

These stories all tie together. **Ultimately it is about the choice between our own desires and the will of the Father.** We choose to do our own thing or we choose to listen to the voice of the Father. We will work in his vineyard or we will follow our own desires. The way we use our resources, including our time, reveals what is in our heart. The one son spoke the right words, but his actions revealed that he was not really interested in the father's vineyard. **Likewise, the institutional church of this day speaks much about serving God, but the actions reveal that the survival and maintenance of the institution is the priority.** The other son repented and did the work for the father. However, the story was not about a father and two sons, but about the Father and his call on the lives of his people for the sake of his Kingdom. Just prior to this, we read about the question asked of Jesus as to who gave him authority to do the work of ministry and his response in asking the leaders what they thought about John the Baptist. They were not willing to answer, for they had rejected John's message in the same way they were doing with Jesus. In fact, let us read what John himself had earlier said to them as recorded in Matthew 3:7-12: *When he saw many of the Pharisees and Sadducees coming to where he was baptizing, he said to them: "You brood of vipers! Who warned you to flee from the coming wrath? Produce fruit in keeping with repentance. And do not think you can say to yourselves, 'We have Abraham as our father.' I tell you that out of these stones God can raise up children for Abraham. The ax is already at the root of the trees, and every tree that does not produce good fruit will be cut down and thrown into the fire. I baptize you with water for repentance. But after me will come one who is more powerful than I, whose sandals I am not fit to carry. He will baptize you with the Holy Spirit and with fire. His winnowing fork is in his hand, and he will clear his threshing floor, gathering his wheat into the barn and burning up the chaff with unquenchable fire."*

Like Jesus, John the Baptist presented the Levitical leadership with a radical challenge as he called them to repentance. He pointedly said that relying on tradition would not help them – it was time to produce fruit. Like the unfruitful fig tree, the Levitical tree was destined to die and to be replaced with the order of Melchizedek. In fact, this was clear when John, a Levite himself, prophesied that there was another coming that would baptize with the Spirit and fire – Jesus, the carpenter from Nazareth from the tribe of Judah. However, those holding religious positions of power did not want to lay these down - while the least likely began entering the Kingdom of heaven ahead of them. This is why Jesus continued by telling the parable we find in Matthew 21:33-46:

Listen to another parable: There was a landowner who planted a vineyard. He put a wall around it, dug a winepress in it and built a watchtower. Then he rented the vineyard to some farmers and went away on a journey. When the harvest time approached, he sent his servants to the tenants to collect his fruit. The tenants seized his servants; they beat one, they killed another and they stoned a third. Then he sent other servants to them, more than the first time, and the tenants treated them the same way. Last of all, he sent his son to them. "They will respect my son," he said.

But when the tenants saw the son, they said to each other: "This is the heir. Come, let us kill him and take his inheritance." So they took him and threw him out of the vineyard and killed him.

Therefore, when the owner of the vineyard comes, what will he do with those tenants?

They replied: "He will bring those wretches to a wretched end and he will rent the vineyard to other tenants, who will give him his share of the crop at harvest time."

Jesus said to them: "Have you never read the Scriptures:

'The stone that the builders rejected has become the capstone;

The Lord has done this and it is marvelous in our eyes.'

Therefore I tell you that the kingdom of God will be taken away from you and given to a people who will produce its fruit. He who falls on this stone will be broken to pieces, but he on whom it falls will be crushed."

When the chief priests and Pharisees heard Jesus' parables, they knew he was talking about them. They looked for a way to arrest him, but they were afraid of the crowd because the people held that he was a prophet.

It is time to listen to these words and to ask the hard questions! In a very real sense the prophetic words of this parable were fulfilled when the leadership arrested Jesus and had him executed on the cross. However, the High Priest in the order of Melchizedek could not be silenced, for he rose from the dead and revealed that he was from eternity to eternity – an eternal High Priest. With this the Levitical order was abolished. The church was birthed on the day of Pentecost when the Spirit was poured out on ordinary people and they were transformed to become royal priests. There was no need and never would be a need for an institution by whatever name where ministry is in the hands and control of a separate class of specially trained priests called clergy. Each person that received Jesus as Lord received the right to become a child of the Father and the risen Lord sent the Holy Spirit to guide each member of his body. Those who know the Good Shepherd hear his voice and do not need a human priest to be an ear and mouthpiece for God's word. Those called to leadership in the body are empowered and anointed to become servants and to share the truth of this new order with every member to equip each one for the work of ministry so that the whole body may work together with each part recognized and released.

This is the issue we face: The church in many parts of the world has chosen to follow the Levitical structure that was fully re-instituted when Constantine was converted. The word spoken by Jesus in the passage above is therefore as applicable today as it was back then. The leadership has taken ownership of the vineyard and will not release the fruit to the owner. The kingdom resources of the Father are being used to build and expand the religious kingdoms in the name of God – whether called church or ministry. Like Israel we have done this so long that we cannot even imagine anything else than the church as institution. In the meantime, the needs of the world are not met and many members are wandering on the barren hills like sheep without a shepherd, while those inside the walls of the churches and their resources are being used to build and maintain the worldly religious kingdoms. The cost factors to keep the doors of the religious buildings open are huge and growing as time passes. The major energy of God's people is spent on keeping the doors open – and when it cannot be done any longer the doors are closed and 'the church' is no more. With this the priority of commitment is to 'our church' and competition is the name of the game in the divisive world of the institutional church. After all, the religious segment of the market is only so big and, in the world of consumer believers, it can be tough for a church to survive. The local priest by whatever title has his/her job cut out – especially since the old denominational commitments are no longer as important as they were a century ago. The yearly budget can make or break a pastoral career and the offerings with their 'tax receipt incentives' are very crucial to keep the doors of many a church open. In this world of the church, stewardship teaching is therefore of vital importance and nothing can rival a church committed to tithing. Let us look at this next.

The Levitical system was supported through the Old Testament laws regarding tithing. This was supplemented at times by offerings over and above the tithe, for example for the upkeep of the temple as we read in 2 Chronicles 24. The tithe served primarily to support the tribe of Levi which had no specific territory and also to care for the orphans, widows and aliens that lived in Israel, as we read in Deuteronomy 15:27-29. Now without getting into all the detail, the key issues need to be noted. First, tithes and offerings in the Levitical system were used to support the Levites (including the priests), to maintain the temple and to support those in need. **Now, most in the institutional church interpret this to mean that tithes and offerings are to be given to the church primarily for the maintenance of the church's property and pastoral (staff) salaries – and a token is given to mission and benevolence toward the needy.** However, when we consider that in Christ the Levitical structure was abolished, it means that with it the need for property and Levitical leadership was abolished. Therefore, if we were able to apply the concept of offerings and tithes as noted above to the church, then it follows that all giving can legitimately only be used for the support of those in need! This is in fact what happened in the early church as we read earlier in the Book of Acts.

But there is more to this: The whole concept of the tithe was part and parcel of the Old Covenant law. However, in Christ the law was fulfilled and we are not under the law, but under grace as Paul wrote to the Romans (see e. g. Romans 6:14 and 15). In Christ we are set free from the slavery of the law and walk in the Spirit as we read in Romans 8:1-4: *There is now no condemnation for those who are in Christ Jesus, because through Christ Jesus the law of the Spirit of life set me free from the law of sin and death. For what the law was powerless to do in that I was weakened by the sinful nature, God did by sending his own Son in the likeness of sinful man to be a sin offering. And so he condemned sin in sinful man, in order that the righteous requirements of the law be fully met in us, who do not live according to the sinful nature but according to the Spirit.* With that, let us turn our attention to Paul's letter to the Galatians. This whole letter was written because they had slipped back from this life in faith, attempting to seek the Spirit through the law by insisting that the believers practice one aspect of the law, circumcision. It is vitally important to understand the implication of re-introducing even just one aspect of the law, as Paul wrote in Galatians 3:10-14: *All who rely on observing the law are under a curse, for it is written: "Cursed is everyone who does not continue to do everything written in the Book of the Law." Clearly no one is justified before God by the law, because "The righteous will live by faith." The law is not based on faith; on the contrary, "The man who does these things will live by them." Christ redeemed us from the curse of the law by becoming a curse for us, for it is written: "Cursed is everyone who is hung on a tree." He redeemed us in order that the blessing given to Abraham might come to the Gentiles through Christ Jesus, so that by faith we might receive the promise of the Spirit.* As Paul continued, he later wrote in Galatians 5:1-3: *It is for freedom that Christ has set us free. Stand firm, then, and do not let yourselves be burdened again by a yoke of slavery. Mark my words! I, Paul, tell you that if you let yourselves be circumcised, Christ will be of no value to you at all. Again I declare to every man who lets himself be circumcised that he is obligated to obey the whole law.* In Christ it is not only the Levitical structure that was abolished and replaced with the order of Melchizedek, but the law itself was fulfilled, the price was paid to set us free from the law as means of accessing God's grace and promises. We live by faith and walk in the freedom of the Spirit. **Thus, to make any part of the law – whether circumcision or tithing – mandatory, means to reject the freedom in Christ and to re-introduce the whole Old Testament law as the only means of salvation. This is the very system that no one could keep and that brought condemnation. Thus, the whole matter of offerings and tithes to be brought to the local church as being the equivalent of the temple (storehouse), brings one under obligation to seek salvation through the works of the law in every way and in the words of Galatians 3:10 it brings us back under the curse.**

It is time to listen to Jesus as we consider this matter of stewardship. His words and actions recorded in Matthew 21 quoted above speak volumes. **The vineyard does not belong to any of us and we do not own even a portion. Everything we have is by the grace of God and given by our Father for the sake of his Kingdom. It is all his and he directs how it should be used as he guides us by the Spirit. It is not about a tithe for him and the rest for us! The tithe was for the Old Covenant with specific instructions (which were often ignored by Israel). The New Covenant way of handling resources is illustrated in a story recorded in Luke 18:18-30:**

A certain ruler asked him: "Good teacher, what must I do to inherit eternal life?" Jesus answered: "Why do you call me good? No one is good, except God alone. You know the commandments: 'Do not commit adultery, do not murder, do not steal, do not give false testimony, honor your father and mother.'"

"All these I have kept since I was a boy," he said.

When Jesus heard this he said: "You still lack one thing. Sell everything you have and give to the poor, and you will have treasure in heaven. Then come, follow me."

When he heard this he became very sad, for he was a man of great wealth. Jesus looked at him and said: "How hard it is for the rich to enter the Kingdom of God. Indeed, it is easier for a camel to go through the eye of a needle than for a rich man to enter the Kingdom of God."

Those who heard this asked, "Who then can be saved?" Jesus replied: "What is impossible with men, is possible with God."

Peter said to him: "We have left all we had to follow you." Jesus said to them: "I tell you the truth, no one who left home or wife or brothers or parents or children for the sake of the Kingdom of God will fail to receive many times as much in this age and, in the age to come, eternal life."

Here is the point: **It all belongs to the Father to begin and all that has been entrusted to us is for the sake of the Kingdom. In the Old Covenant a tithe was required to be given with some additional offerings, but in the New Covenant we do not give God a measly 10% - we give everything! Our example is set by Jesus Christ of whom we read in 2 Corinthians 8:9:** *For you know the grace of our Lord, Jesus Christ, that though he was rich, yet for your sake he became poor, so that you through his poverty might become rich.*

It is really important to understand this as we follow Jesus. In the words of Philippians 2:5-11: *Your attitude should be the same as that of Christ Jesus:*

Who being in the very nature of God, did not consider equality with God something to hold onto, but made himself nothing, taking the very nature of a servant, being made in human likeness. And being found in the appearance as a man, he humbled himself and became obedient to death, yes death on a cross!

Therefore God exalted him to the highest place and gave him the name that is above every name, that at the name of Jesus every knee should bow, in heaven and on earth and under the earth, and every tongue confess that Jesus Christ is Lord, to the glory of God the Father.

Let us now begin to connect the dots to see the picture. It is not about a portion – whether 10% or more or less! Jesus did not set aside 10% of his divinity for the sake of the Kingdom. He willingly gave it all away to become a servant and then as a servant he gave all he had, even his life! **In this he illustrated a key principle of the Kingdom: What we hold onto, we loose, but what we give away for the sake of the Kingdom, we gain. This is the principle underlying the well-known words: Seek first the Kingdom of heaven and its righteousness and all the things (food, clothing and shelter) that you need will be given to you. This is the key to understanding the concept of servant hood in the New Covenant, as we read in John 12:23-26:** *Jesus replied: "The hour has come for the Son of Man to be glorified. I tell you the truth, unless a kernel of wheat falls to the ground and dies, it remains only a single seed. But if it dies, it produces many seeds. The man who loves his life will lose it, while the man who hates his life in this world will keep it for eternal life. Whoever serves me must follow me; and where I am my servant will also be. My Father will honor the one who serves me."*

The story of the rich young ruler quoted earlier is the key to understanding stewardship in the New Covenant. All we have belongs to the Father. When he directs us to do something with whatever he has entrusted to us, we are to obey – even if it does not make sense to us. We like all our nice little rules and regulations and principles to guide us in our giving, buried in our understanding of 'being responsible in how we handle God's gifts.' We use these to undermine and deny the radical words of Jesus and to soften the impact, for we do not want people to walk away like the rich young man. We really do not want to alienate potential givers, especially those with many resources! In fact, this is why we teach people to give 10% (or even soften that to be less) to the church (meaning local Institution), for it is much more palatable than to challenge them with the truth. We like to be able to fit God's word into our little boxes constructed with human logic, but as Isaiah 55:8-9 says: *"For my thoughts are not your thoughts, neither are your ways my ways," declares the Lord. "As the heavens are higher than the earth, so are my ways higher than your ways and my thoughts than your thoughts."* In fact, it is really enlightening to listen to Jesus and look at him dealing with these matters to see that our little logical boxes do not fit his way of looking at resources.

Matthew 17:24-27 relates the following: *After Jesus and his disciples arrived in Capernaum, the collectors of the two-drachma tax came to Peter and asked, "Doesn't your teacher pay the temple tax?" "Yes, he does," he replied.*

When Peter came into the house, Jesus was the first to speak. "What do you think, Simon?" he asked. "From whom do the kings of the earth collect duty and taxes – from their own sons or from others?"

"From others," Peter answered.

"Then the sons are exempt," Jesus said to him. "But so that we may not offend them, go to the lake and throw out your line. Take the first fish you catch; open its mouth and you will find a four-drachma coin. Take it and give it to them for my tax and yours."

The tax here referred to the annually collected funds required of every Jewish male 20 years of age or older and it was used for the upkeep of the temple. It is similar to an institutional church's collection for the 'building or maintenance fund' except that in the church we do not normally tax people but expect the support through voluntary giving. Knowing what Peter had said, Jesus asked him the question whether a king's son would pay tax in the kingdom or whether he would tax others. The answer was obvious and we can see Jesus with a twinkle in the eye adding that in the Kingdom of God the sons should also be exempt. **In a real sense he did free us as children of God from the burden to build and maintain earthly sanctuaries, for God could never and would never be confined to a structure made by human hands. Instead, he chose to make his people the new temple as Paul wrote in 1 Corinthians 3:16-17:** *Don't you know that you are God's temple and that God's Spirit lives in you? If anyone destroys God's temple, God will destroy him; for God's* *temple is sacred, and you are that temple.* However, rather than argue the point and offend them, Jesus sent Peter to go fishing, open the first fish's mouth and he would find a coin exactly worth what was required of him and Jesus to pay the tax. **Again, let us not miss this. Those who live in dependence on the Father and seek his Kingdom will find that their needs will be met – even in miraculous ways.**

Matthew 20:1-16 is the story of workers hired at different hours to work in the vineyard. Incidentally, this story follows Matthew's version of the story of the rich young ruler and it puts a Kingdom perspective to the challenge of handling Kingdom resources. Let us read this story.

For the Kingdom of heaven is like a landowner who went out early in the morning to hire men to work in his vineyard. He agreed to pay them a denarius for the day and sent them into his vineyard. About the third hour he went out and saw others standing in the marketplace doing nothing. He told them, "You also go and work in my vineyard and I will pay you whatever is right." So they went. He went out again the sixth hour and the ninth hour and did the same thing. About the eleventh hour he went out and still found others standing around. He asked them: "Why have you been standing here all day long doing nothing?" "Because no one has hired us," they answered. He said to them: "You also go and work in my vineyard."

When evening came the owner of the vineyard said to his foreman: "Call the workers and pay them their wages, beginning with the last ones hired and going to the first.

The workers who were hired about the eleventh hour came and each received a denarius. So when those came who were hired first, they expected to receive more. But each one of them also received a denarius. When they received it, they began to grumble against the landowner. "These men who were hired last worked only an hour," they said, "and you have made them equal to us who have borne the burden of the work and the heat of the day!"

But he answered one of them, "Friend, I am not being unfair to you. Didn't you agree to work for a denarius? Take your pay and go. I want to give the man who was hired last the same as I gave you. Don't I have the right to do what I want with my own money? Or are you envious because I am generous?" So the last will be first and the first will be last.

Without going into a detailed discussion, it is important to note a few key things in the story. First, the landowner was not unfair, but simply displayed a liberal generosity towards those who started later. Second, in doing this he obviously thought differently than the human logic of most as voiced by the man who complained. In the context of Jesus' time the story addressed the issue of those who had been serving God for a long time compared to relative new comers. This is not much different than the way we often treat one another in the church, giving positions and power to 'longstanding members' and expecting new comers to first prove themselves worthy. **However, the key issue is to note once again that the land (and resources) is owned by the landowner and he can do what he wants with the resources, even giving liberally**

to those who do not deserve it when viewed through our eyes. Our Father is generous! His generosity exceeds our human ways of thinking and when we are entrusted with resources, we need to keep this in mind. Much of what is taught in church regarding stewardship misses this point entirely, for we want to be 'responsible.' By this we simply mean we want to determine if the recipient of our handout measures up to our standards and like those in the story who worked through the day, we are less charitable than the owner and even begrudge his generosity to others.

With this it is time to move to yet another story, this time not one told by Jesus, but something that happened to him. This story is recorded in every one of the four gospels. Let us read it as written in Mark 14:1-9:

Now the Passover and the Feast of Unleavened Bread were only two days away, and the chief priests and the teachers of the law were looking at some sly way to arrest Jesus and kill him. "But not during the feast," they said, "or the people may riot."

While he was in Bethany, reclining at the table of a man known as Simon the Leper, a woman came with an alabaster jar of very expensive perfume, made of pure nard. She broke the jar and poured the perfume on his head. Some of those present were saying indignantly to one another, "Why this waste of perfume? It could have been sold for more than a year's wages and the money given to the poor." And they rebuked her harshly.

"Leave her alone," Jesus said. "Why are you bothering her? She has done a beautiful thing to me. The poor you will always have with you and you can help them at any time you want. But you will not always have me. She did what she could. She poured perfume on my body beforehand to prepare for my burial. I tell you the truth, wherever the gospel is preached throughout the world, what she has done will also be told, in memory of her."

Let us get right to the heart of the matter: In very real terms those who criticized the woman represent 'responsible stewardship' as practiced and taught in most churches (except that in today's churches it would not be spent on the poor, but on buildings, programs and salaries). In terms of 'responsible stewardship' this act was nothing but extravagant waste. **However, Jesus obviously thought differently and expressed it clearly. What made no sense to those who witnessed this act, was indeed a sacrificial investment in the Kingdom in preparing the body of the Lord for his burial. The key to this woman's Kingdom investment was a spontaneous act of love towards Jesus with no reservations. Her love for Jesus broke the confinement of controlled giving to release all she had saved in overflowing generosity to minister to his needs and in this process her life was transformed by his love and grace.**

With this in mind, let us consider the fact that we meet this same Jesus every day in different situations where we have the opportunity to minister to him. He comes to us in the person in need that crosses our path – whatever the need may be. This is what Matthew 25:31-46 is all about: *When the Son of Man comes in his glory, and all the angels with him, he will sit on his throne in heavenly glory. All the nations will be gathered before him and he will separate the people one from another as a shepherd separates the sheep from the goats. He will put the sheep on his right and the goats on his left.*

Then the King will say to those on his right: "Come, you who are blessed by my Father; take your inheritance, the kingdom prepared for you since the creation of the world. For I was hungry, and you gave me something to eat; I was thirsty and you gave me something to drink; I was a stranger and you invited me in; I needed clothes and you clothed me; I was sick, and you looked after me; I was in prison and you came to visit me."

Then the righteous will answer him: "Lord, when did we see you hungry and feed you, or thirsty and gave you something to drink? When did we see you a stranger and invite you in or needing clothes and clothe you? When did we see you sick or in prison and go to visit you?"

The King will reply: "I tell you the truth, whatever you did for one of the least of these brothers of mine, you did for me!"

Then he will say to those on his left: "Depart from me, you who are cursed into the eternal fire prepared for the devil and his angels. For I was hungry and you gave me nothing to eat; I was thirsty and you gave me nothing to drink; I was a stranger and you did not invite me in; I needed clothes and you did not clothe me; I was sick and in prison and you did not look after me."

They also will answer: "Lord, when did we see you hungry or thirsty or a stranger or needing clothes or sick or in prison, and did not help you?"

He will reply: "I tell you the truth, whatever you did not do for one of the least of these, you did not do for me." Then they will go away to eternal punishment, but the righteous to eternal life.

It is time to face some facts. Our churches with the buildings, programs and salaries of the Levitical staff members are the vases filled with the precious resources entrusted to us by our Father. These vases are worshiped and treasured and we make sure there is a narrow bottle neck so we only pour a few drops at a time when we see need and it only comes from the overflow. The narrow bottleneck is the stewardship teaching that only releases the occasional overflow into a controlled program that fails to address the vast needs around us. Like the overseers and teachers of the law at the temple, the church leadership of this day is upset when one dares to overturn some of the tables and question the waste of resources to run the church machine. When the Lord shows up in the poor and needy, support if any is a drop from the narrow neck called "benevolence." More likely those in need coming to church will not receive anything, except be handed an envelope for giving to support the church with a promise of a blessing depending on their giving! The Levitical structure of the church and ministries has effectively monopolized the resources in believers' hands to be used primarily for the needs of the institutions. All the teaching on Kingdom resources focuses on giving to the institutions first, to such an extent that for most members spontaneity is reduced to giving over and above what they had planned for the offering.

The truth of the matter is that there are more than adequate resources in the hands of believers today to literally change the world. The only thing holding us back is the fact that most believers do not walk in the Spirit with the mindset of the early church in this area. Most hold onto the resources as if they actually own them and have settled for the lie that a portion belongs to God (that is to the institutional church) and the rest is for them. What is given ends up in the hands of those that have a vested interest in the institution and pour it into this vase with the small neck so that little is available for those in need. Therefore, spontaneous generosity that flows from the heart is virtually lost within the body of believers and occasionally, when it happens, it is almost exclusively from the overflow. Some do recognize that all we have belongs to God and that spontaneous generosity and hospitality are vital aspects of our faith, but for the most part this is a mental exercise and rarely a lifestyle practice as it was in the early church. When reading Matthew 25 few of us expect that Jesus does actually confront us in the person in need on a regular basis.

When we personally walked out of the world of the church, God began to open our eyes and teach us these lessons in a very real way. It was a process through which we learned to live by faith and totally depend on the Father for our provision as we moved into an itinerant ministry. In this process much of what I shared earlier became revealed to us and in obedience to God's word we chose not to build a ministry in the way of the world of the church, but simply to walk in faith. God further gave me specific assignments in prayer and these had to be pursued full-time, even though I did not receive any specific support to do this ministry. Very few people understood what we were doing and from a logical point of view it made no sense. From time to time we found ourselves in need in ways we had never before experienced and for the first time in our lives we walked in the shoes of the needy. At one point I realized that we had become a prophetic challenge to many in the church – both to friends and to others that knew us. In a word, the Christ in us presented them with the reality of needs that could be met if they chose to do that. Some did and we have amazing stories of generosity and love as they reached out to touch our lives. The vast majority, however, did not know how to handle us and we tasted first-hand what many people experience from the church when they face needs.

At the same time, we were learning key lessons ourselves and we were being challenged in ways we never imagined possible. God had linked me with businessmen with a Kingdom vision and in time we developed a vision of intercessory ministry for Kingdom business. In the pursuit of this vision they lost all they had and walked the same path with us, seeking a breakthrough. The Lord also gave us a name for our ministry at the time, Breakthrough Prayer Ministries. So we faced the reality that we have this name and the very business for which we prayed for years had not only not experienced the breakthrough, but also lost everything! We developed a model of intercession in business and even though we believed God led us in this, there seemed to have been no fruit. We received key prophetic words and rarely wavered in faith as we battled in the Spirit with these words, but seemingly nothing was gained. In seeking investment funds for the dream, God linked us with three specific individuals and for over more than 10 years the majority of my time was spent praying for them and their work – with no obvious breakthrough and no investment funds that came forth. As we prayed, we came to know these men with their hopes and dreams, but also their weaknesses and their needs. God revealed to us that our investment in the Kingdom was first and foremost an investment in the lives of these people. He was more concerned with their lives than with the millions that they could potentially raise and invest in the Kingdom. This lesson really hit home as one of them at a crucial time for him and for us suddenly died and everything we had worked for disappeared in a split second. The only thing we had was the fact that Jim's relationship with the Lord was changed and restored, because we spent time with a lonely man following a dream. We did not gain one penny in investment for the

Kingdom, but we have the treasure in heaven of a friend whose life we could touch for the Lord. Likewise, the prayer for the second friend has not brought any major investment for the Kingdom after more than 10 years of intense and specific prayers.

As we prayed and battled with no breakthroughs and with challenges to survive amidst dwindling resources and little income, we faced all kinds of temptations to make things happen. I asked myself many questions (and was asked the same by others): "Did I really hear this correctly from the Lord? Does it make sense to continue the process, as there is seemingly no breakthrough? Shouldn't I at least find even just a part time job to supplement our income in order to survive or at least be sensible and follow the path of successful ministries by raising funds and selling resources instead of giving these away? Am I faithfully persevering or is it just stubborn pride that keeps me from accepting the inevitable?" In fact, I battled with the Lord about these things many times, but to no avail. In the midst of this we did see the hand of God in wonderful ways and learned to live on a very limited income – disgraced at times because of the lack we faced on a daily basis. However, the real test was to come in the person of the third man for whom we prayed, a prodigal son struggling to find his way home.

I am not at liberty to share much, except to say that this man was and to this day remains a real test to many others and to us. At one time early in our journey we called him Waldo for at the time you never knew where in the world he was. In his journey as a prodigal he made numerous enemies and often had to run. There were rumors of money issues and legal battles. Waldo was a schemer and always in need of funds and during the time we got involved a small fortune was spent to keep him going, with the promise that the big breakthrough is at hand. After two years, money and time spent, he walked away as he was unwilling to change at the time. We released him to the Lord wherever he was and did not hear from him for about a year. When he returned it was a carbon copy of the previous time with same issues and a similar game plan, except that God spoke to us and we sensed this was for real and we were to walk with him to the end. What seemed as it would be a short journey of a few weeks turned into over 7 years where we walked extra mile after extra mile. During this time the Lord did his miracles and our friend changed in a powerful way. Hidden agendas were revealed and unrighteous ties severed. In the process we were confronted with injustice and manipulation and abuse of power even where we least expected it, as the enemy resisted his release. The long battle included legal fees and expenses that were far greater than we could imagine, especially as things were dragged out by the abuse of power. God supplied in these needs in ways that we could not have imagined and we kept marveling at the miracles we saw – but it was not easy – especially when he chose to be Waldo again!

On a personal level we were challenged to give in a major way at a time when we could least afford it. In fact, we were not even making it ourselves when God had us pour into this man. We could relate to the story of the widow being challenged by Elijah to first prepare him a meal from her last flour and oil, trusting that the God of Israel would provide for her and her son's needs according to the prophet's words. So month after month we poured out – falling behind in key areas. As we listened to the Lord, it made no sense, but we determined that if it cost us our house, we will obey the Lord to help set the captive free and we literally faced that. As the cold weather set in, we were faced with the choice to help the man or have the gas cut off, leaving us without hot water or able to use our furnace and God said to give it away. We expected that it would not be too long, but it dragged on and we endured some amazingly cold Canadian days and nights with a few small electric heaters that we moved around the house. In time we faced the reality that we had to put our house up for sale as a result of our choice to help this brother and we had to give our house away. In the midst of this journey we faced the celebration of Easter with barely enough to get a small meal and struggling to survive the weekend. A year later we faced the same again, this time after we had given away all that we received from the sale of our house to the project with a brother in need! These were only some of the challenges we faced as we gave and gave yet again and we were not the only ones doing this. During this time, we had many join with us in prayer for him and to see him back in the Father's house and we spent hours and days in prayer for him – it was literally a full time job to pray for him.

To many believers and friends what we did made no sense and they were not willing to give any support. In fact, to most that call themselves "Christians," intense prayer seems to be a total waste. To many what we did and still do is a waste of time and resources. The reality is that most believers choose not to invest in a ministry where prayer for a single individual might be considered a full-time job! It offends the logic of being responsible! To claim that God directed this sound like lunacy, especially when there seems to be no result and let us face it, the effectiveness of prayer is not easy to evaluate. James 5:17-18 says: *Elijah was a man just like us. He prayed earnestly that it would not rain, and it did not rain on the land for three and a half years. Again he prayed, and the heavens gave rain, and the earth produced its crops.* Now, Elijah's prayers did bring results that were seen as effective, **but between these prayers he spent three and a half years in hiding, most of them living in a little room in a heathen woman's house with nothing to do but trust for a daily miracle to have a meal. In terms of human logic, this was a tremendous waste of his anointing and call – and his living arrangement certainly did not pass the religious tests.** In fact, most of the Biblical characters that are rightly viewed as examples of faith spent years with little to show in terms of success! Would you e. g. have invested in Noah's ship building yard?

Before we conclude this chapter on freedom to handle resources, let us look at one other Biblical example, the story recorded in 1 Samuel 15. King Saul is sent to battle the Amalekites and is told to totally destroy everything that belongs to them and not spare anyone or anything. He attacks with his army and wins the battle, but they spared Agag, the king, and the best animals. Upon his return Saul is confronted by the prophet Samuel and asked why he disobeyed. His response was that he did what he was told to do, but simply took their king captive and saved the best animals as a sacrifice to the Lord. Then we read the following words in 1 Samuel 15:22-23: *But Samuel replied: "Does the Lord delight in burnt offerings and sacrifices as much as obeying the voice of the Lord? To obey is better than sacrifice and to heed is better than the fat of rams. For rebellion is like the sin of divination and arrogance like the evil of idolatry. Because you have rejected the voice of the Lord, he has rejected you as king."* What the Lord expected seemed to have been a total waste of resources! Saul took matters into his own hand and made a logical decision that really made sense. Why senselessly destroy what could be valuable to the kingdom? **Yet his disobedience cost him the kingship!**

It is time to close this chapter and connect the dots to see the picture. Actually, it is simple! **The freedom to handle the Kingdom resources entrusted to us flows from the recognition that we own nothing! Every single thing we have belongs to the King and he has the power and authority to direct when and how it is to be used. He does this through his Spirit setting up divine appointments for each member of his body to touch the lives of others through whom we meet**

the King himself. As we do this, we invest in the Kingdom of God in which the priority is the lives of people for whom he gave his own life. As God's people we are set free to be generous, even to give all away, for the Father will meet our needs as we seek his Kingdom first. All we need to do is to listen to the Spirit and be obedient in handling the resources, even when it does not make sense to us!

The key resources in the Kingdom are people. This is why the Levitical structures are so wasteful. These structures do not only waste resources in terms of time and money to keep the institutions going, but they waste the precious resource of God's people by tying them to the pews (or chairs), forever running programs to keep God's people sitting, listening and giving the offerings to keep the system going. Each person in this world has been ordained before the creation of this world to be a unique member of the body of Christ, equipped by the Spirit to do the work of ministry. This is why the key task of leaders is to equip God's people for their work of ministry and to release them to do that. In this leaders are to serve the people and not use them to build institutions to provide their income. They are to trust the Father to meet their needs as they seek first his Kingdom and train people to hear the voice of God. God directs us by the Spirit to the needs he wants each of us to meet. Thus it is not about a portion first to "my church," and thereafter to some other organization when I feel like it. Kingdom giving flows out of the heart and more often than not it is a spontaneous act. Even when Paul was taking a special offering for the needy, he advised in 2 Corinthians 9:7 that *"each man should give what he has decided in his heart to give, not reluctantly or under compulsion, for God loves a cheerful giver."* All our giving should be in obedience to the guidance of the Spirit and is inherently a personal decision.

When we moved out of the institutional church and started planting house churches and encouraging others to do the same, we did not expect these to become the source of our income. In fact, we set people free and encouraged them to seek the Lord as they invest in the Kingdom of heaven. We never take an offering, but those coming to the church at our home are true givers. Their eyes have been opened and they have become Kingdom givers, willing to give beyond expectation and not just a portion of the overflow. They give from the heart, often spontaneously and with great generosity. They are the ones who will break the vase and pour it all out with no reservation. I am praying for the day when the church will once again be filled with Kingdom givers so that there will not be one whose needs are not met. I believe there is a day approaching when the people of God will see a great transfer of wealth into the Kingdom and will lead the way to meet the needs of the world with wisdom that will astound the world. However, before that becomes a reality, we will need to learn to be faithful with the resources that are in the hands of believers now. That will only happen when God's people are free to hear his voice and to be carried by the Spirit. Let us pursue that.

BORN AGAIN TO BE FREE LIKE THE WIND

I grew up in an evangelical home and tradition. There was no doubt that one had to be born again to enter the Kingdom. Our understanding of these terms was not different from that of most evangelicals in North America. To be born again one prayed the sinner's prayer in repentance, accepted the Lord and then joined a Bible believing church.

The Lord has taught me to be sensitive to little things that happen to me and how they are often related to one another. Sometimes I would be led to read a book – or re-read a chapter, someone shares a word or a dream and suddenly there is a revelation that I never expected. A while back Eda was at a conference where Don Potter was the speaker. She came home with his CD, "Since the Fall," and as I listened to it, I was struck by a particular song. Interestingly enough, it was just at the time that I was led to meditate on the freedom of the Spirit. Let us begin by reading the words of this song entitled "Born again, again."

Sometimes I feel like I was saved
to the church – and not to you.
At times I feel like my service is
to everyone else – but you.

In my strife to please man – I've
failed to please you.
Through my struggles to be
accepted – I denied acceptance
from you.

I want to be born again, again.
Go all the way back to my first
love and then
finally believe your loving-kindness
has no end.
I want to be born again, born
again, again.

I was lured by her weakness -
and in my own strength tried
to set her free,
but I lost myself in her daily
dues – and her endless needs.

In my efforts to edify her -
I only exalted me.
I was closer to the body than I
was to the head and that can

never be.

No more condemnation -
I am going to fight for the
next generation
to be free from this
false obligation
and walk in the power of
true reformation.

I want to be born again, again.
Go all the way back to my first
love and then,
finally love your bride the way
you intend.
I want to be born again, born
again, again.

This song challenged me to think about the term "born again" as we often use it. As I did this, I realized that the emphasis is more on our connection to the institutional church than to the Lord. We 'hear' the word of the Lord through the preaching, we 'grow' in faith through our endless Bible Studies, we join in 'fellowship' through our small groups and social activities, we 'serve' the Lord through the programs in church, we 'submit' to the Lord by being accountable to the leadership and we are 'in unity' with those who share our doctrinal positions. Many (most notably leaders) who claim to be "born again" rarely spend any personal time with the Lord and most do not know how to hear his voice. They once repeated the sinner's prayer and became members of the local church and that is the extent of their faith. In the light of how we often use the term "born again" it is very interesting to actually read the key passage where this term is found in the Scriptures, John 3:1-8: *Now, there was a man of the Pharisees named Nicodemus, a member of the Jewish ruling council. He came to Jesus at night and said: "Rabbi, we know you are a teacher who has come from God. For no one could perform the miraculous signs you are doing if God were not with him. In reply Jesus declared: "I tell you the truth, no one can see the Kingdom of God unless he is born again." "How can a man be born when he is old?" Nicodemus asked. "Surely, he cannot enter a second time into his mother's womb to be born?" Jesus answered, "I tell you the truth, no one can enter the Kingdom of God, unless he is born of water and the Spirit. Flesh gives birth to flesh, but the Spirit gives birth to spirit. You should not be surprised at my saying, 'You must be born again.' The wind blows wherever it pleases. You hear its sound, but you cannot tell where it comes from or where it is going. So it is with everyone born of the Spirit."*

As the conversation developed from there Jesus explained to Nicodemus the way to salvation in John 3:16-17: *For God so loved the world that he gave his one and only Son, that whoever believes in him shall not perish, but have eternal life. For God did not send his Son into the world to condemn the world, but to save the world through him.* It is therefore correct to say that to be "born again" one must have accepted Jesus as personal savior. In the words of Romans 10:9-10: *if you confess with your mouth, "Jesus is Lord" and believe in your heart that God raised him from the dead, you will be saved. For it is with your heart that you believe and are justified, and it is with your mouth that you confess and are saved.* **Thus, the sinner's prayer is part and parcel of salvation and being "born again." However, in the process one becomes part of the body of Christ, the church. We do not join the church, but are joined to the church! Note that Jesus did not tell Nicodemus that once a person is "born again" he has to find a church and become a member. What he said was that such a person is as unpredictable as the wind, for he is led by the Spirit.**

It is important to take a close look at this picture. The point of comparison is the fact that we do not control the wind. We can observe its presence and feel it, but we do not control the wind. We cannot make it blow or stop. The person who is born again is like that, in other words, is someone who is under the influence of the Spirit of God and not subject to another person's control. We can see the work and presence of the Spirit, but cannot direct when and how the Spirit may work in and through the one who is born again. **Thus, to be "born again" is not just to pray the sinner's prayer and "join a Bible believing church." To be born again is to accept Jesus as Lord and to be filled with the Spirit to the point of becoming as unpredictable as the wind.** We will return to this point shortly, but first need to turn to the Book of Acts to illustrate this again.

In Acts 19:1-7 we read the following interesting story: *While Apollos was at Corinth, Paul took the road through the interior and arrived at Ephesus. There he found some disciples and asked them: "Did you receive the Holy Spirit when you believed?" They answered, "No, we have not even heard that there is a Holy Spirit." So Paul asked, "Then what baptism did you receive?" "John's baptism," they answered. Paul said, "John's baptism was a baptism of repentance. He told the people to believe in the one coming after him, that is, in Jesus." On hearing this they were baptized into the name of the Lord Jesus. When Paul placed his hands on them, the Holy Spirit came on them and they spoke in tongues and prophesied. There were about twelve men in all.*

Let us look at this story again. Paul arrived in Ephesus and met disciples. As he spent time with them, he found there was something not quite right, for the presence of the Spirit in their lives was not evident. To understand this, we need to look to the previous chapter. In Acts 18:24-26 we read: *Meanwhile a Jew named Apollos, a native of Alexandria, came to Ephesus. He was a learned man with a thorough knowledge of the Scriptures. He had been instructed in the way of the Lord and he spoke with great fervor. He taught about Jesus accurately, though he knew only the baptism of John. He began to speak boldly in the synagogue. When Priscilla and Aquila heard him, they invited him to their home and explained to him the way of the Lord more adequately.*

The men Paul met were likely believers that Apollos had led to faith and baptized prior to his meeting with Aquila and Priscilla. Thus, when Paul met them, he found that they were true believers, but something was not right. Note his key question: "Did you receive the Holy Spirit when you believed?" This question ties in with the words Jesus spoke to Nicodemus when he said: *"I tell you the truth, no man can enter the Kingdom of God, unless he is born of water and the Spirit."* **Baptism with water as an act of faith in Christ is tied to the baptism of the Spirit.** In fact, this was the key to the birth of the church as recorded in the Book of Acts. To be "born again" did not simply mean that a person had made a decision for Jesus and was baptized as sign of this step of faith, but it meant the person was filled with the Spirit and the presence of the Spirit was evident in the life of that person. **It is time to pursue this further in the Book of Acts, for this is the key to seeing why our way of church has become so empty and why there is such a lack of power in the church.**

In the opening chapter of Acts, Luke tells Theophilus that in the first book (that is the Gospel of Luke) he endeavored to tell the story of the life, death and resurrection of Jesus. The Book of Acts is the continuing story of the church that is the body of which the resurrected Christ is the head. Setting the stage in Acts 1:4-8 Luke wrote: *On one occasion while Jesus was eating with them, he gave them this command: "Do not leave Jerusalem, but wait for the gift my Father promised, which you have heard me speak about. For John baptized with water, but you will be baptized with the Holy Spirit." So when they met together, they asked him, "Lord, are you at this time going to restore the Kingdom to Israel?" He said to them, "It is not for you to know the times or dates the Father has set by his own authority. But you will receive power when the Holy Spirit comes on you; and you will be my witnesses in Jerusalem, in Judea and Samaria and to the ends of the world."* As the story unfolds, we find that they heeded the command of Jesus and prayerfully waited in Jerusalem. Then we read the following in Acts 2:1-4: *When the day of Pentecost came, they were all together in one place. Suddenly a sound like the blowing of a violent wind came from heaven and filled the whole house where they were sitting. They saw what looked like tongues of fire that separated and came to rest on each of them. All of them were filled with the Holy Spirit and began to speak in other tongues as the Spirit enabled them.*

This act of the Spirit opened the door for an empowered Peter to preach to the crowd that came to see what was going on and he quoted the words of Joel 2:28-32 to explain the outpouring of the Spirit to those who assembled: "*In the last days," God says, "I will pour out my Spirit on all people. Your sons and daughters will prophesy, your young men will see visions and your old men will dream dreams. Even on my servants, both men and women, I will pour out my Spirit in those days, and they will prophesy. I will show wonders in the heaven above and signs on the earth below, blood and fire and billows of smoke. The sun will be turned to darkness and the moon to blood, before the coming of the great and glorious day of the Lord. And everyone who calls on the name of the Lord will be saved."* At the conclusion of his preaching many asked what they should do and Peter responded in the words of Acts 2:38-39: *Repent and be baptized, every one of you, in the name of Jesus Christ for the forgiveness of your sins. And you will receive the gift of the Holy Spirit. The promise is for you and for your children and all who are far off – for all whom the Lord our God will call.*

As we continue to read, we find that those who believed were baptized and 3000 were added to the church that day. This is a pattern through the book of Acts and the key to the power and effectiveness of the early church. **In a nutshell, the believers were filled by the Spirit and walked in the Spirit. To be "born again" was to believe in Jesus and the Spirit baptized those who believed. They were recognized by the presence of the Spirit of God in their lives that showed in the fruit of the Spirit and also in the manifestation of the gifts of the Spirit.** This is why Paul asked the question about the Spirit to the disciples he met in Ephesus. The lack of the presence of the Spirit in their lives was obvious to him. So, they were baptized in the name of Jesus and he laid hands on them, they received the Spirit and spoke in tongues and prophesied. **Prior to that point they had repented and believed in Jesus, but they were not filled with the Spirit. It was only after Paul laid his hands on them that they were filled with the Spirit and received the gift promised by the Father.**

In a real sense the disciples that Paul met at Ephesus were no different from the vast majority of evangelical Christians today. They had their 'denominational connection' with John the Baptist, Apollos led them to the Lord, they repented and they believed in Jesus. They were baptized in water, but had no experience of the power and presence of the Spirit. That was not good enough for Paul and he asked the crucial question as we saw above. **However, today in the church we have settled for this watered-down interpretation of "born again" and it is little more than a cultural way of life. In truth most of our baptisms are in actuality 'the baptism of John', in water but not in the Spirit.** It is interesting to read Paul's warning to Timothy that in the last days many will turn from the faith and fall in all kinds of sin, **having a form of godliness, but denying its power.** It is time to ask the serious question and be born again, again! It is time to be born again and restore the cracked foundations of our faith, so that we move like the wind similar to the early believers, as recorded in the Book of Acts.

When we read the story of the early church in the Book of Acts, we find that the Spirit moved them. In the words of Jesus to Nicodemus, the early believers were like the wind. It started on the day of Pentecost when they heard the sound and each one was baptized in the Spirit. They moved out of the house into the street where the church was birthed and they kept moving. This was prophetic for the church. The wind of the Spirit could not and would not be contained in a building from that point on. The old was gone and the new had come. The temple of the old covenant was replaced with the temple of the new covenant, which is the body of believers filled with and guided by the Spirit. Even with the dedication of the first temple, in 2 Chronicles 6:18 Solomon declared: *"But will God really dwell on earth with men? The heavens, even the highest heavens, cannot contain you. How much less this temple I have built!"* The new temple would not be of mortar and stone, but the Lord would build it with the living stones of Spirit filled believers. It took a while for the new reality to set in, especially as the first believers were all Jewish and the temple building was still standing in Jerusalem. However, persecution moved them beyond the walls of Jerusalem into Judea, then into Samaria and thereafter they set their sights on the world itself. In this process they were moved and directed by the Spirit, for they were born again to be like the wind.

In the pages of the New Testament we discover a people who walked in a freedom that many today cannot imagine. As we have seen when we looked at their way of handling resources, they were able to let go of everything and no one considered that they owned anything. They were willing to freely give away to others in need so that every member's needs were met. Jesus' words in John 8:36, *"If the Son sets you free, you will be free indeed,"* became a reality in the lives of those who believed. They were baptized not just with water, but with the Spirit of the Lord. As Paul wrote in 2 Corinthians 3:17, *now the Lord is Spirit and where the Spirit of the Lord is, there is freedom.* The story of the early church in the Book of Acts is the story of people who moved in freedom. They were like the wind – willing to move wherever and with no hesitation. They were able to change course and even walk away from successful ventures when they heard the Spirit. They were able to change positions and mindsets in the face of religious tradition as they listened to the Spirit. They were willing to suffer and even to die for their faith, in obedience to the Spirit. They saw miracles and walked in power and authority as they followed the Spirit. Leaders became true servants and ordinary people were equipped and set free to do the work of ministry, as the old Levitical order was replaced with the order of Melchizedek.

That freedom was lost when the church was changed under Constantine to become an institution and with that the priesthood of the believer was replaced by re-instituting a "Christianized Levitical priesthood." The unity of the body of Christ, the church, was broken as settled clergy replaced the itinerant servant leaders and the rest of the body became subservient to them as laity. Members stopped to function in the body as they submitted to the clergy instead of obeying the Spirit. The temple that Jesus built with living stones was cast aside and replaced with cathedrals and churches built with human hands using bricks and mortar and the resources of the Kingdom were diverted to local kingdoms where men ruled. As the walls were built with mortar and stones and the spiritual wall between clergy and laity was erected, the wind of the Spirit was blocked from moving in the church. The Reformation recovered the Word of God in Scripture and with that revelation began to flow and to challenge the Levitical traditions, but to this day the key issues have not been addressed, because both people and leaders in the Levitical institutions fear the freedom of the Spirit. It is time to deal with this fear and its roots.

There are a number of reasons why most people in church shy away from dealing with the issues mentioned above. There is a fear of change, for the religious spirits working through tradition have conditioned most to settle for the status quo. Much of the teaching in churches is focused first on keeping people in the pew and second to make sure they support the local church and its traditions. The leaders are trained in Levitical thought patterns and paid to maintain the status quo. They are dependent on the income from the local church and most will not risk losing this income base by letting go of their positions and the power and control vested in these positions. Leaders fear releasing people to be blown by the wind of the Spirit, unless they somehow have control over them. The people in the pew have been conditioned to pay clergy to do the ministry and are not willing to invest all they have in a relationship with Christ where the Spirit of God is in control. Most people do not want the responsibility to listen to the Spirit and would rather "do the religious thing as expected," than walk in the freedom of the Spirit. With this, we are getting to the heart of the issue, which is a fear of the Spirit and fear of the freedom of the Spirit, despite all the denial even by many "Spirit filled" believers.

As we read in John 3:8 Jesus said: *"The wind blows wherever it pleases. You hear its sound, but you cannot tell where it comes from or where it is going. So it is with everyone born of the Spirit."* **The issue is our willingness to let go of our control and trust the Spirit to guide us.** I am not talking about many who have 'membership' in the church, but for whom the Spirit is nothing more than an empty word or part of the creed. There are many who are deeply committed to the religious structure of the institutional church who are totally unwilling to even consider the possibility that the Holy Spirit is a living person and that they need to be born again. They fear the Spirit, because they do not want to be part of the "charismatic world and its chaos." They only talk about the Spirit in intellectual terms and do not have or wish to have any experiential knowledge of the Spirit. Again, I am not talking about them. I am talking about the believers who have accepted the Spirit and consider themselves as "Spirit filled believers." The fact is that despite all the talk in many such circles and churches of being open to the Spirit and willing to move with the Spirit, most do not trust the Spirit to lead the church. We still have our four walls and occasionally open a window to let the wind bring a breath of fresh air in, but we like to control the opening and closing of the window. **We like to invite the Spirit to move as long as we control the movement. That is why we have all the leadership controls in place with the "appropriate teaching on submission to human leaders," for we do not trust the Spirit. In a word, we like to use the wind as long as**

we are in control of the sails of our church-ship with the hand on the rudder. However, Jesus said in plain words that those born of the Spirit are as unpredictable as the wind!

As I read the story of the church in the Book of Acts, I find a body directed by the head, Jesus, through his Spirit. The whole story of Acts is the story of the people moving with the wind of the Spirit. In fact, the book is not about the Acts of the Apostles, but it is about the Acts of the Spirit. **The key to understanding the role of the leaders in the Book of Acts is to recognize that the one thing they were concerned about was that the disciples were filled with the Spirit. The leaders knew that then and only then could the believers do the work of ministry and move with the wind.** We already looked at the birth of the church on the day of Pentecost when the small group of disciples were filled with the Spirit and following the sermon by Peter he told the crowd in Acts 2:38-39: *Repent and be baptized, every one of you, in the name of Jesus Christ for the forgiveness of your sins. And you will receive the gift of the Holy Spirit. The promise is for you and for your children and for all who are far off – for all whom the Lord our God will call.* As the Spirit moved them their actions were spontaneous and lives were changed, for example the miracle at the temple gate when a crippled man was healed. When questioned about this, empowered by the Spirit, Peter and John stood with boldness in the presence of the Sanhedrin and refused to yield to pressure to stop moving in the

Spirit. They met with the other believers and prayed for more boldness and then we read in Acts 4:31: *After they prayed, the place where they were meeting was shaken. And they were all filled with the Spirit and spoke the word of the Lord boldly.* Ananias and Sapphira tested the Spirit and died. Persecution then scattered the believers and they spread the message in word and deed as they moved away from Jerusalem.

It is here that we see the focus of the apostolic leaders on the presence and power of the Spirit. Philip moves into a city in Samaria and through the Spirit many lives are changed, people are set free and many believe. Then we read in Acts 8:14-18: *When the apostles in Jerusalem heard that Samaria had accepted the word of God, they sent Peter and John to them. When they arrived, they prayed for them that they might receive the Holy Spirit, because the Holy Spirit had not yet come upon any of them; they had simply been baptized into the name of the Lord Jesus. Then Peter and John prayed and laid hands on them, and they received the Holy Spirit.* Following this they rebuked Simon the Sorcerer for he offered them money for the power to lay hands on people to receive the Spirit. After this, they returned to Jerusalem, preaching in other cities on the way back. **Please note what did and what did not happen: The apostles did not take over or even advised Philip how he should do the work. They did not appoint a resident pastor or pastoral team nor did they even organize the new church with buildings and programs. They simply made sure that the new believers were filled with the**

Spirit (just like Paul later did with the disciples in Ephesus as we saw earlier) and trusted the Spirit to guide them! Thus, once they were filled with the Spirit, relatively new believers were left on their own by the apostles.

Let us turn to the first letter of John to get the picture. In the second chapter of this letter John wrote specific words of advice to three groups within the church: the new believers whom he called "children," the mature members whom he called "young men" and the fathers in the faith that he appropriately called "fathers." Following that he focused on the "children" (verse 18 and following) and in verse 20 he wrote, *"But you have an anointing from the Holy One and all of you know the truth."* In other words, they were filled with the Spirit of whom Jesus said that he would lead us in the truth. Admonishing them to stay in the truth, John then writes the following in 1 John 2:26-27: *"I am writing these things to you about those who are trying to lead you astray. As for you, the anointing you received from him remains in you, and you do not need anyone to teach you. But as the anointing teaches you about all things and as that anointing is real, not counterfeit – just as it has taught you, remain in him."* **Once believers were filled with the Spirit, the apostles had no problem releasing them to walk in the Spirit. They did not have to be organized and placed under Levitical leadership to guide and keep them for fear that they will not survive.** It was not just John's opinion! His partner in the mission to Samaria as we know was Peter. It is very enlightening to read 2 Peter 1:3-11 where he wrote to the believers who received a faith as precious as his own: *The divine power of Jesus has given us everything we need for life and godliness, through our knowledge of him who called us by his own glory and goodness. Through these he has given us his very great and precious promises, so that through them you may participate in the divine nature and escape the corruption of the world caused by evil desires. For this very reason, make every effort to add to your faith goodness; and to goodness, knowledge; and to knowledge, self-control; and to self-control, perseverance; and to perseverance, godliness; and to godliness, brotherly kindness; and to brotherly kindness, love. For if you possess these qualities in increasing measure, they will keep you from being ineffective and unproductive in your knowledge of our Lord Jesus Christ. But if anyone does not have them, he is near-sighted and blind; and he has forgotten that he has been cleansed from his past sins. Therefore, my brothers, be all the more eager to make your calling and election sure. For if you do these things, you will never fall, and you will receive a rich welcome into the eternal kingdom of our Lord and Savior Jesus Christ.* John and Peter were not alone in holding this opinion. In Romans 15:14 Paul wrote to the believers in Rome: *I myself am convinced, my brothers, that you yourselves are full of goodness, complete in knowledge and competent to instruct one another.* These words were written to believers that were mostly uneducated slaves, yet Paul had no hesitation to believe that they could minister adequately and effectively to one another!

However we want to read the passages above, they do indicate that Peter, John and Paul believed that the Holy Spirit is fully

capable (and better equipped than human leaders, whatever their positions, titles, denominational affiliations, training, etc. may be) to lead the church. Real leadership ensured that members were born again by water and the Spirit and then trusted the Spirit to guide each member. This was a pattern in the early church. This is why Paul could plant a church and often move on quickly and the church would survive and thrive. The Lord builds his church and the more we move out of the way, the better it is. The wind of the Spirit often does not make sense in our human mindsets, thus our tendency to try and control the lives of people. It is fascinating to see that the early church did not have the same problem. They moved with the wind of the Spirit and did not question it or seek the opinion of a leader or another believer when they heard the voice of God. In fact, the story of Philip in Samaria illustrates very well. In the midst of the powerful move of the Spirit where he was leading the revival, confirmed and blessed by the apostles, an angel told him to pack up and go to a lonely desert road. **With no hesitation he left and walked away from the success and followed the wind of the Spirit to this road where he met an Ethiopian eunuch and we read in Acts 8:29,** *the Spirit told him, "Go to that chariot and stay near it."* As he did an opportunity arose to share the gospel and baptize this man and with that the message of Jesus spread and the roots of the church was laid in Ethiopia. Moved by the wind of the Spirit Philip disappeared from the

Ethiopian's sight and appeared in Azotus. Interesting too is that the Ethiopian man did not need anything else but that brief meeting to be equipped to lay the foundations of the church in his country!

We find example after example of this in the Book of Acts. In Acts 9 the key persecutor of the believers meets the risen Lord in the dust of the road to Damascus. Physically blinded by this encounter, he is led into the city and taken to a home where he stayed for three days. The wind of the Spirit then blew into the home of a man by the name of Ananias who was directed in a vision to the specific house to lay hands on Saul and pray for him. Upon his question about this, God spoke to Ananias and told him that he had chosen Saul to become a major instrument in the Kingdom. **Without hesitation and without checking with other believers for a second opinion or getting a blessing from a local pastor, he went to the address, found Saul, laid hands on him and prayed. Saul's eyesight was restored and Ananias baptized him and introduced him to the other disciples. Immediately Saul started preaching the gospel!**

The next story in Acts is the story of Cornelius. Like Philip he was directed by an angel to send for Peter and like Ananias he was given precise directions to the house where Peter stayed in Joppa. At the same time the wind of the Spirit blew into the house and Peter had a vision that challenged the very core of his being as a Jewish believer, being directed to eat food that he had considered to be unclean. This vision prepared him for what was to follow as we read in Acts 10:19: *While Peter was still thinking about the vision, the Spirit said to him: "Simon, three men are looking for you. So get up and go downstairs. Do not hesitate to go with them, for I have sent them."* **With no hesitation Peter met with them and the next day traveled to Cornelius' house where he preached the gospel. Even as religious Jew he did not hesitate to enter the Gentile house, for he had heard the Spirit and in obedience shared the message of the gospel.** In the house of Cornelius there was an even greater surprise for Peter and his circumcised friends, for Acts 10:44-48 reports that *while Peter was still speaking these words, the Holy Spirit came on all who heard the message. The circumcised believers who had come with Peter were astonished that the gift of the Holy Spirit had been poured out even on the Gentiles. For they heard them speaking in tongues and praising God. Then Peter said: "Can anyone keeping these people from being baptized in water? They have received the Holy Spirit just as we have." So he ordered that they be baptized in the name of Jesus Christ. Then they asked Peter to stay with them for a few days.*

Again, however we want to read this story, the fact is that the Holy Spirit initiated it and Peter and his companions walked in obedience, even though in their natural minds as religious Jewish believers everything in them would have said they should not have done so. In fact, when the word reached the other Jewish believers, we read in Acts 11:2-3 that they criticized Peter and said, *"You went into the house of uncircumcised men and ate with them."* It is very important to read the rest of this, for it tells us that Peter then related what had happened from the beginning to the end, concluding with Acts 11:15 -17: *As I began to speak, the Holy Spirit came on them as he had come on us at the beginning. Then I remembered what the Lord had said: "John baptized with water, but you will be baptized with the Holy Spirit." So if God gave them the same gift as he gave us, who believed in the Lord Jesus Christ, who was I to think that I could oppose God?* **Then we read the response of the critics, Acts 11:18:** *When they heard this, they had no further objections and praised God saying, "So then, God has granted even the Gentiles repentance to life!"* **The only thing that mattered to them was the evidence of the presence of the Spirit!**

As we look at this story it is also very important to note what was not done! Peter stayed for a few days only and then left! He did not organize the new church and did not appoint a resident pastor. He somehow was not concerned that they may need regular teaching by a trained theologian! **He simply trusted the Spirit to guide the believers!** He also did not make sure that they were connected to 'his church in Jerusalem' nor did he suggest that they become accountable to the 'apostolic leaders' and seek 'a covering' for this new church. **The wind of the Spirit blew him into the house, worked through him and blew him out. The Spirit who made it happen was in charge and they were connected in the Spirit**

and covered by the presence of God. Nothing more was needed.

The next story in Acts records the breeze of the Spirit through the work of ordinary believers scattered through persecution to various parts of the region, including Antioch. Like Peter the Spirit guided some to speak to Gentiles and they responded. Then we read in Acts 11:22-24 that *news of this reached the ears of the church in Jerusalem and they sent Barnabas to Antioch. When he arrived and saw the evidence of the grace of God, he was glad and encouraged them all to remain true to the Lord with all their hearts. He was a good man, full of the Holy Spirit and faith, and a great number of people were brought to the Lord*. We do not know what "the evidence of God's grace" referred to, but a guess would be that it showed in the presence of the Spirit in the lives of the believers. What is important is to see yet again that Barnabas did not try to take control or re-organize the church, but simply encouraged them. It is also worth our while to note that he was seen as "a good man, full of the Holy Spirit and faith." As the story unfolds Barnabas brought Paul to Antioch and this now becomes a major center of the faith as the church grew in numbers. How this was managed is not clear, except that we do know the early Christians had no church buildings with central programs. It would be reasonable to assume that they met in homes and occasionally gathered in larger groups with the house churches joining together. Various leaders are mentioned in Acts 13 and we learn that there were prophets and teachers among them.

Then we read the following in Acts 13:2-4: *While they were worshiping the Lord and fasting, the Holy Spirit said, "Set apart for me Barnabas and Saul for the work to which I have called them." So after they had fasted and prayed, they placed their hands on them and sent them off. The two of them, sent on their way by the Holy Spirit, went down to Seleucia and sailed from there to Cyprus.* **Again, we find that the Holy Spirit led the church. The wind of the breath of God directed the mission of Paul and Barnabas and as the story unfolds, we read how Paul, filled with the Spirit, spoke a word and the sorcerer Elymas was blinded for a time. This miracle opened the door to faith for the proconsul at Cyprus. They continued through opposition and persecution,** *filled with joy and the Holy Spirit* **(Acts 13:52) and were successful and** *spoke boldly for the Lord, who confirmed the message of his grace by enabling them to do miraculous signs and wonders* (Acts 14:3). Upon their return they *gathered the church together in Antioch and reported all that God had done through them and how he had opened the door of faith to the Gentiles.*

Throughout the Book of Acts it is clear that the early church was nothing else than a body of believers moving as the Spirit guided them. When they needed to make decisions, there was only one question: "What does the Spirit say?" In fact, as we continue through the book, the next chapter records the story of the council at Jerusalem where leaders and members from Antioch traveled to the city to

meet with the apostles and elders about the debate regarding circumcision. As we read the story, they concluded that Gentiles did not need to be circumcised. This decision followed the address by Peter relating how the Spirit fell on the Gentiles as it did on them in the beginning, showing that God accepted them as he did the Jews. Then Barnabas and Paul told them how God had done miracles among the Gentiles as they shared the message of the Kingdom. The fact that the Spirit was at work among the uncircumcised Gentiles was the real proof that enabled them to make the decision that it was not necessary to insist that they be circumcised.

We can continue through the rest of the Book of Acts and we will find more confirmation of what we observed above. The Spirit guided the believers and therefore it was of vital importance to them that new believers were baptized in water **and the Spirit**. The evidence of the baptism in the Spirit was often observed in the fact that they spoke in tongues and prophesied. Once filled with the Spirit, leaders had little trouble releasing even new believers to walk in the freedom of the Spirit. There is not one shred of evidence that the apostles or other leaders appointed or required a church to have a resident pastor to oversee the local body. The oversight was entrusted to the Spirit and left in the hands of the church with the elders (mature leaders) taking leadership. However, this oversight by elders was also under the direction of the

Holy Spirit, for we read how Paul in his last words to the elders in Ephesus told them in Acts 20:28-31: *"Keep watch over yourselves and all the flock of which the Holy Spirit has made you overseers. Be shepherds of the church of God that he bought with his own blood. I know that after I leave, savage wolves will come in among you and will not spare the flock. Even from your own number men will arise and distort the truth in order to draw away disciples after them. Be on guard. Remember that for three years I never stopped warning each of you night and day with tears."* Paul's whole ministry and every one of his mission journeys were the result of listening to the Spirit. In the end, even when it made no sense in the natural, he followed the Spirit to Jerusalem where he was arrested and imprisoned. He did not hesitate or shrink back when it was revealed to him that it would happen. In the process he eventually, after years, went to Rome as a prisoner and it allowed him to reach the very heart of the Roman Empire with the gospel.

This is the point: The early church made an impact and changed their world, because they followed the Spirit's direction. The Spirit filled the members of the church and the leaders released them to the wind of the Spirit to be blown wherever the Spirit moved. They walked in divine power and authority with humility and grace, submitted to the Lord and following the Spirit. They traveled lightly, for earthly possessions were not important to them. They trusted the Father to provide in their needs. They were generous and hospitality was practiced by all, opening homes to travelers and to itinerant leaders, directed by the Spirit. As the message was preached new believers were added to the church daily, for the message was confirmed by signs and wonders through the power of the Spirit. This is in sharp contrast to the way the Levitical church functions, for it is based on human organization. This is clearly illustrated by our church planting methods compared to what we see in the Book of Acts. Paul never did a survey to find where the best place would be to start a church; he never needed the approval of an overseeing denominational body and the support it offers; he did not ever seek the right location for the church building and the funds to erect any such structures; he never served as senior pastor or appointed a settled pastor to take over once he left, etc. **As we walked out of the world of the church, the freedom of the Spirit became more and more real to us. We became free to move with the Spirit and set free from pleasing men. With this the control issues were removed and as we continued, we learned that the Spirit is indeed far more capable to lead the church than we could ever be! Today we easily release people and trust the Spirit. We minister as the Spirit leads and where he opens the door – at times in surprising ways and places. We are free to speak the word of the Lord with candor and integrity and minister wherever there is need. We are able to touch lives where the church program can never function. It is about the willingness to be obedient to the Spirit and to move with the wind of the Spirit.**

When I was in the world of the church, I saw the church as a sailboat or sailing ship. Those of us who were serious about the Holy Spirit would try to discern the breeze of the Spirit and set the sails accordingly in order to be carried to the destination. The leadership determined the destination and coordinated the work to move the vessel to where we want to be. On the ship some are passengers who come along for the ride and they are often the majority! However, they pay the dues that are needed to keep the ship afloat and pay the salaries of the captain and crew. As such they have power and often determine the direction of the ship and its destination. Most ships do the same journey on a yearly basis and offer the favorite repeat programs and designated ports for stops. Most are family cruise oriented and the key needs are the operating funds and programs to keep the various family needs covered with a focus on different age and gender groups. From time to time the ship will take on new passengers or crewmembers, mostly transfers from another vessel. The captains also move to other vessels when opportunity arises (or sometimes are thrown overboard or set adrift by disgruntled passengers and crew). The bigger the ship, the more power and prestige to be on board and especially to lead it. In the world of the church as in the natural world, the sails have in many ways given way to engines and the ship does not need to rely on the wind!

As we were moved out of the world of the church, I began to think about these things differently. For one thing, I recalled the joy of spending three days with our family on a sailboat on Georgian Bay in Lake Huron. It was amazing and relaxing – especially as our friends did the work! However, I learned a few things about sailing and one of them is that we can actually sail into the wind. **Applying this to the picture above, it means that we can use the power of the Spirit and the word of God to navigate our church ship against the direction of the wind. This is what commonly happens in many churches where the human leadership controls actually shut down the breeze of the Spirit. This is also why so many that move powerfully in the Spirit can fall into deep sin. The issue is not one about power, but about obedience and yielding to the Spirit.** As he ended the Sermon on the Mount, Jesus spoke about recognizing a tree by its fruit and warned against the false prophets. Then he added, Matthew 7:21-23: *Not everyone who says to me, "Lord, Lord," will enter the Kingdom of heaven, but only he who does the will of my Father in heaven. Many will say to me on that day, "Lord, Lord, did we not prophesy in your name and in your name drive out demons and perform many miracles?" Then I will tell them plainly, "I never knew you. Away from me, you evildoers!"* It is not about the manifestation of power by using (and abusing) the wind of the Spirit. Many churches and ministries are built in this way – great sailing vessels using the power of the wind, but sailing into the wind!

Before we look at another picture, we need to heed a warning from Scripture. I believe we are in a prophetic time of challenge and change for the church that will be unprecedented in scope. The current breeze, which many interpret as God's favor, will change and the man-made Levitical designed and operated ships will not survive. **We are moving into the third day of our Lord – the third millennium. The words of Jesus when he was warned against Herod were not only a reference to his death and resurrection, but also a prophetic word about his church. In Luke 13:32-33 we read:** *Go, tell that fox, I will drive out demons and heal people, today and tomorrow* *and on the third day I will reach my goal (perfect my church).* *In any case, I must keep going today and tomorrow and the next day, for surely, no prophet can die outside Jerusalem.* The stage is being set for our Lord to perfect his church. He will be returning for a pure and spotless bride. Much of what has been built is nothing but human empires and pyramids – built upon the sand. All man-made structures and their controls will be broken. Many a majestic ship will be wrecked when the power of the Spirit is released. In fact, there is an interesting story in the Book of Acts that pictures this in an amazing way. In Acts 27 Luke records this story. A word from the Lord to Paul set the stage for the journey: While he was imprisoned in Jerusalem, we read in Acts 23:11 that *the following night the Lord stood near Paul and said: "Take courage. As you have testified about me in Jerusalem, so you must also testify in Rome."* As Paul found, God's prophetic words often take much longer to become a reality than what we anticipate. However, the words that he would go to Rome to witness continued to carry him and strengthen his faith amidst the storms that he encountered.

More than 2 years later after many trials and imprisonment, Paul, who had appealed to Caesar, was on his way to Rome. After some time, they ran into difficult sailing conditions and landed at Myra where they boarded an Alexandrian ship sailing for Italy. Again, with difficulty they battled the conditions and had to change course and sail to the lee of Crete where they arrived at Fair Havens. Then we read the following in Acts 27:9-12: *Much time had been lost and sailing had already become dangerous, because by now it was after the Fast. So Paul warned them: "Men, I see that our voyage is going to be disastrous and bring great loss to ship and cargo, and to our lives also." But the centurion, instead of listening to what Paul said, followed the advice of the pilot and the owner of the ship. Since the harbor was unsuitable to winter in, the majority decided that we should sail on, hoping to reach Phoenix and winter there. This was a harbor in Crete, facing both southwest and northwest.*

Let us get to the point: It became late for sailing and even as they made progress, they encountered conditions that slowed them considerably. **Prophetically we are entering a season where the old ways will not move us forward. There are warning signs all over for those who listen to the Spirit. However, many in the church are like the centurion. They take their cues from the Levitical leadership who have a vested interest in the ship, like the pilot and the owner in the story. So, they take a vote and the majority rules. The problem with this is that the Kingdom of God is not a democracy for He is the King and He rules!**

Let those who have ears hear what the Spirit is saying to the church!

The story continues in Acts 27:13-20 we read that "*when a gentle south wind began to blow, they thought they had obtained what they wanted; so they weighed anchor and sailed along the shore of Crete. Before long a wind of hurricane strength, called the "northeaster," swept down from the island. The ship was caught by the storm and could not head into the wind; so we gave way to it and were driven along. As we passed the lee of a small island called Cauda, we were hardly able to make the lifeboat secure. When the men had hoisted it aboard, they passed ropes under the ship itself to hold it together. Fearing they would run aground on the sandbars of Syrtis, they lowered the sea anchor and let the ship be driven along. We took such a violent battering from the storm that the next day they began to throw the cargo overboard. On the third day, they threw the ship's tackle overboard with their own hands. When neither sun nor stars appeared for many days and the storm continued raging, we finally gave up all hope of being saved.*" Like the sailors on the ship, many in the church mistakenly set sail to reach their chosen destination when they sense a breeze! **Many mistake the presence of the Spirit for God's approval of their plans and set out in presumption, unwilling to listen to the prophetic words of those who are not part of the inner circle. After all, what did Paul know about sailing a ship?** We are entering a season in the Spirit where there is a change in the direction and force of the wind. The latter rain of the Spirit is about to fall and the houses built upon the sand of human interpretations will be washed away. The Spirit of God will come in a way and from a direction that few on board the church ships can imagine. The least likely ordinary people will hear the Spirit and walk in a power that will defy the Levitical leadership and the churches with their controls will not be able to handle the storm unleashed by the order of Melchizedek. It will not be possible to fight this movement of the Spirit. In the end the churches will experience the power of God's Spirit and will be forced to acknowledge it. Like the crew and passengers on this ship, they will try different things to keep the ship afloat – give way to the Spirit, try to secure lifeboats (the teachings and statements of faith), lower the anchors (try to regain control) and discard some of the programs and baggage of administrative controls, even some things they never thought they would let go (the tackle). Finally, they will give up the fight to regain control and loose hope. **That is the point that God will open the door – when man will acknowledge his inability to control the power of the Spirit and the move of God.**

In the story at the point when they were in despair for their lives, the prophet whose word they had rejected spoke forth words of hope for we read in Acts 27:21-26: *After the men had gone a long time without food, Paul stood up before them and said: "Men, you should have taken my advice not to sail from Crete; then you would have spared yourselves this damage and loss. But now I urge you to keep up your courage, because not one of you will be lost; only the ship will be destroyed. Last night an angel of the God whose I am and whom I serve stood beside me and said: 'Do not be afraid, Paul. You must stand trial before Caesar; and God has graciously given you the lives of all who sail with you.' So keep up your courage, men, for I have faith in God that it will happen just as he told me. Nevertheless, we must run aground on some island."* Again, this is a prophetic word for the church of this day: As in this story with Paul, God's prophetic word will not return empty! He is building his church and the gates of hell will not stand against it. He will perfect his body, the church, and before he returns his bride will be without spot or wrinkle. Around the world the prophetic words are confirming the message and there is going to be major change in the church. We will return to this shortly, but first have to continue with the story as it unfolds in Acts 27:27-44.

After two weeks of being battered by the storm, they sensed that they were approaching land. The sailors tried to get onto the lifeboat and leave the rest, but Paul again spoke to the centurion and they dropped the plan and cut away the lifeboat. With the changes coming amidst the storm our lifeboats and plans will not work and will have to be abandoned. After that Paul encouraged them to eat and took the lead, taking bread and giving thanks to God. They ate and then again lightened the load by throwing even the grain into the sea. When daylight came, they did not recognize the land! **The future is going to be unfamiliar territory for the church, for the wind of the Spirit will take us to the unknown places where our feet have not walked before!** With the land close by and the wind blowing, they decided to run the ship aground in the sandy beach if they could. They did, but the bow stuck fast and the stern was broken to pieces by the pounding surf. Paul's presence brought favor to the other prisoners and those that could swim swam ashore and the rest held onto planks and pieces of the ship. Everyone reached the land safely.

Now most in the church will not even understand what is being said, for they do not have any experiential knowledge of the Spirit and neither of the gift of prophecy. However, those who do and many prophetic voices of our day readily admit and expect that the church of the future will be vastly different from the world of the church as it is generally known in the western world. There is a general sense in the Spirit that there will be an outpouring of the Spirit that will be of a magnitude never seen before, with the church walking in power and authority like the early believers and with the blessing of God that will release huge resources for the Kingdom. **I truly believe that we are entering this season for the church. However, the vast majority of the prophetic voices of our day have not wrestled with the possibility that the church as we generally know it may not only be radically changed, but may not survive at all! Most are so conditioned by the model of the institutional church that they automatically assume that it will remain and simply be empowered by the Spirit. In a word: Many assume that the ocean will be filled with more boats and ships of the various denominational**

and "non-denominational" fleets fishing the waters and pulling in the nets! Even the mere suggestion that the church as we know it, like the Alexandrian ship in Acts 27, will not just be battered and forced to discard the baggage and equipment, but will ultimately be destroyed, is seen by many as an attack on the church. It is not! It is simply the recognition that the end-time church will return to its roots and the Levitical structure that was imposed upon the church changing it from a living organism to a dead organization, will be discarded. The order of Melchizedek with Jesus as High Priest and every member of his body functioning as a royal priest cannot be expressed in the old Levitical covenant model. In the words of Hebrews 8:13, *by calling this covenant "new," Jesus made the first obsolete; and what is obsolete and aging, will soon disappear.*

As I said above, many people totally misunderstand us when we say that the church as we know it will not just be changed, but it will not survive. The concept of the church in the western mindset is so tied to an institutional understanding that most in the church cannot fathom what the Spirit is saying today. It is like the time when the people of God associated the temple in Jerusalem with the presence of God and totally rejected the prophetic warnings of Jeremiah about the coming destruction of Jerusalem. In the words of Jeremiah 7:3-4 the prophet warned them, *this is what the Lord Almighty, the God of Israel says: "Reform your ways and your actions, and I will let you live in this place. Do not trust in deceptive words and say: 'This is the temple of the Lord, the temple of the Lord, the temple of the Lord.'"* As that story unfolded Jeremiah eventually ended up as prisoner, because they rejected the warnings. However, the prophetic word did not return empty and Jerusalem and the temple were demolished. Years later Jesus spoke similar warnings to his disciples regarding the temple that was rebuilt by the exiles and later expanded by Herod the Great, as we read in Luke 21:5-6. Referring to his body, as recorded in John 2:19, he also said, *"Destroy this temple, and I will raise it again in three days."* These words were used as 'evidence' against him when he was tried by the Jewish leaders as we read in Matthew 26:60-67. He was put to death on the cross, but his words did not return empty and in three days he rose from the grave and in the year 70 the temple in Jerusalem was demolished never to be rebuilt.

These words are warnings to the church that we cannot simply assume that God will not destroy the church as we know and practice it! In Jeremiah 18:1-6 there is an amazing illustration that we need to heed: *This is the word that came to Jeremiah from the Lord: "Go to the potter's house and there I will give you my message." So I went down to the potter's house and I saw him working at the wheel. But the pot he was shaping from the clay was marred in his hands; so the potter formed it into another pot, shaping it as it seemed best to him. Then the word of the Lord came to me: "O house of Israel, can I not do with you as the potter does?" declares the Lord. "Like clay in the hand of the potter, so are you in my hand, o house of Israel."* Later on, in verses 11-18, the prophet spoke forth yet again the words of judgment against Israel and they rejected the warning. **Here is the issue: In the same way as potter God can not only remove the Levitical church and form it into the order of Melchizedek, but he will. The assumption of many that because the church has functioned in the Levitical structure for centuries, it will continue in this way to the end, is nothing but wishful thinking. God's word will not return empty and the end-time church will be restored to the order of Melchizedek. The reason many reject this as too radical is that they are so close to the structure, they cannot see it in perspective. The view from a distance is very different than from close up! Ultimately the question is whether or not we know the Spirit well enough to trust him fully to lead the church!**

As we walked out of the world of the church many Scriptures came alive as the Spirit began to speak in new ways. To return to the beginning of this chapter, the whole concept of being "born again" radically changed my mindset. The old pictures did not fit any more. As we began to encounter many believers wandering on the hills like sheep without a shepherd, we ministered to them and saw lives changed. When they were empowered by the Spirit and released, they began to move in the breeze and became like the wind. Now as we did this we knew that the five-fold leadership gifts to the church (apostles, prophets, evangelists, pastors and teachers) according to Ephesians 4:12-13 is given *to prepare God's people for works of ministry, so that the body of Christ may be built up until we all reach unity in the faith and in the knowledge of the Son of God and become mature, attaining to the whole measure of the fullness of Christ.* The whole idea is that those called to these offices are to equip the saints for their work of ministry and the logical next step is to set them free to do this ministry. As we saw in the Book of Acts the key task of equipping was to ensure that they were truly born again, that is filled with the Spirit, and then released to move wherever the Spirit may take them.

With this being said, it is very enlightening to read the next verses in this letter, Ephesians 4:14-16. They explain in more detail the concepts mentioned before as follows: *Then we will no longer be infants, tossed back and forth by the waves, and blown here and there by every wind of teaching and by the men in their deceitful scheming. Instead, speaking the truth in love, we will in all things grow up into him who is the Head, that is Christ. From him the whole body, joined and held together by every supporting ligament, grows and builds itself up in love, as each part does its work.* The idea is very clear that the task of the leaders to equip the saints for their work of ministry is to get them filled with the Spirit and able to hear and respond to the Spirit. **We have a choice: the breath of God, the Spirit, will blow us, or we will be blown by the winds of human teaching. The human teaching is visibly displayed throughout the church in the**

denominational divisions, each with its own distinctive teaching! So, we have the seas filled with all kinds of ships and boats, fleets and individual vessels under specific flags, based on 'the teachings of our traditions.' Sometimes there are greater or smaller alliances bringing limited cooperation. The sails are set according to the teachings and at times the ships tack against the wind of the Spirit.

As we walked out of the world of the church, these observations became more visible than ever. With that a radically new picture was formed in my spirit: **Could it be that rather than ships on the ocean, it is more correct to view the church simply as the collection of leaves that have died and fallen from the trees and are driven by the wind?** To be honest, when compared to the picture of majestic ships and boats on the ocean being handled by purpose driven anointed and skilled crewmembers, the picture of leaves blowing in the wind does not look very impressive! After all, it would seem to be much closer to the words "driven by every wind of teaching" that we quoted above and thus changing direction as the wind does. **However, the key question is the one of control. I am not talking about the "winds of the teachings of men," but the wind of the Spirit!** We are impressed by human organization and charismatic and purpose driven leaders and people can accomplish much. There is an interesting story in Genesis 11 about the power of purpose driven people working in unity to build a city and a tower that would reach to the heavens to make a name for themselves and not be scattered over the face of the earth. It is amazing to read in Genesis 11:6 that God himself said: *"If as one people speaking the same language, they have begun to do this, then nothing they plan to do will be impossible for them."* The issue is one of control. We like to use the power of the Spirit, but struggle to yield to him. We are impressed by human organization and skill and would quickly follow a strong anointed leader. Thus, most of us relate better to being on a sailboat than being compared to a leaf being blown around by the wind!

It is time for those with ears to hear, to listen to the Spirit. The early church members resembled leaves being driven by the wind of the Spirit far more than people on ships piloted by trained and equipped theologians and leaders who set sails and handle the rudders of local churches, as many today consider essential. They did not win the world by being well organized and under direction of seminary trained theologians able to dissect the Biblical text and add all kinds of interesting facts from the world of knowledge to make their point. They were simply ordinary people moved by the Spirit and acting in the name of Jesus to touch lives, like Peter and John who healed the cripple at the temple gate and when brought before the Jewish leaders that had Jesus crucified, boldly proclaimed the gospel. Following this we read in Acts 4:13, *when they saw the courage of John and Peter and realized that they were unschooled, ordinary men, they were astonished and they took* *note that they had been with Jesus.* We also see this in 1 Corinthians 1:26-29 where we read: *Brothers, think of what you were when you were called. Not many of you were wise by human standards; not many were influential; not many were of noble birth. But God chose the foolish things of the world to shame the wise; God chose the weak things of the world to shame the strong. He chose the lowly things of this world and the despised things – and the things that are not – to nullify the things that are, so that no one may boast before him.* **Like leaves in the fall the early believers were willing to let go of the security they had on earth and be blown by the wind of the Spirit whatever the direction may be. They were willing to be taken by the wind of the Spirit and to give their very lives to enrich the soil and bring blessings in the name of Jesus. Like leaves they were blown into groups where they were with others and then some would be blown away again on another mission. The only thing that mattered was that they moved with the Spirit and that the Spirit was in them and working through them.**

Many in the church who are open to the Spirit have yet to fully embrace the Spirit. There is a fear of the Spirit, covered underneath a wet blanket called "order," which usually is nothing but control by insecure people. Often the moving of the Spirit looks chaotic and without purpose to us, like the blowing of leaves in the wind. Leaders (and others) are afraid of those who move quickly and readily when the Spirit stirs. They are often called "loose cannons" and "those who need to learn to submit". Moreover, the wind of the Spirit seldom fits our little boxes and rarely ever makes sense to our minds. Thus, we are challenged by those who say, "God told me to..." and without asking permission or advice, just go ahead and do it. Leaders in the church especially have a very hard time with those labeled "intercessors." The label is wrong, for there is no gift of intercession. Intercessors are those who flow in the prophetic and see things, which often include the hidden agendas and actions which the leadership do not want others to know about. They pray effectively with insight and power, because they see in the Spirit and this leads to the label "intercessor." They therefore scare the living daylights out of many in leadership in the institutional churches, because they see in the Spirit and know what is hidden. The sad part is that most of them are not released in freedom to do their prophetic ministry and as a result the wind of the Spirit is cut off from moving in the church to a large degree. **However, the wind of the Spirit is stirring and ordinary people will experience this and move with boldness, breaking the chains that bind them to the pews controlled by insecure leadership. They will become like Peter and John who told the Jewish leadership in Acts 4:19-20,** *"Judge for yourselves whether it is right in God's sight to obey you rather than God. For we cannot help speaking about what we have seen or heard."* Sometimes it will not look orderly to those who do not trust the Spirit, but those who trust him will see beyond the natural in the Spirit and will not try to wrestle for control. Furthermore, as the intensity of the move of the Spirit increases, the rising tide of those who have been set free will not be controlled by insecure leaders anymore. Those who have tasted this freedom in the Spirit will move with the Spirit and the ships of Levitical control will not survive.

Here is the key issue: You will be driven by the Spirit or you will submit to human agendas, however anointed or off base they may be. The choice is yours! You are called to be a royal priest in the order of Melchizedek, serving the Lord in the freedom of the Spirit and yielded to his will. However, you can choose to reject this and have someone else try to represent you before God as an old order Levitical priest. Yes, you can reject the privilege to listen to the Spirit and choose to be on a religious ship chartered by human leaders on the ocean of life driven by winds of doctrine.

Ultimately it comes down to a matter of trust and the question is whom do you trust more, the Spirit or the leader who decides what the Spirit is saying! As we look at this it is vital to address the concern raised by those who are blinded by the Levitical model that they are used to. The concern is that by allowing each person to hear the Spirit for himself and to follow his voice, it will lead to utter chaos, for not all hear clearly. It is true that not all hear clearly! However, there is no guarantee that a leader will hear any better than any other person! So, if I miss it on my own, I will make a mistake, but if the pastor misses it, the whole church will make a mistake. I do not deny that many will make mistakes – but it happens regularly in the leadership of the Institutional Church today. Submission to human leaders simply magnifies the effects of such mistakes. Furthermore, when mistakes are made, I have seen and personally trust that the Spirit is better equipped to bring restoration, healing and even correction in the situation than any human leader. **Our journey out of the world of the church became a journey out of the world of manipulation and control and out of the battles that these things bring. As we learned to walk in the freedom of the Spirit, we found a security that released us to let go of the control over people. The flip side of this coin was that we learned to trust the Spirit to speak to ordinary people and to guide them in all truth as Jesus said in John 16:13. So we were able to release people easily, even to make mistakes! We saw the Spirit bring conviction as Jesus said in John 16:8 where we would have brought condemnation! The more we moved out of the control mode, the more we saw the Spirit move and lives changed as people were released to respond to the voice of God without needing input from leaders. The less we became, the more Jesus became! The more he became, the more secure we were and the more freedom we experienced – and the easier it became to set others free to be driven by the wind of the Spirit. In the words of 2**

Corinthians 3:17 and Galatians 5:1, *"the Lord is Spirit and where the Spirit of the Lord is, there is freedom"* and *"it is for freedom that Christ has set us free. Stand firm then and do not let yourselves be burdened again by a yoke of slavery!"*

As we move into this new millennium the wind of the Spirit is gaining in strength. The church ships built with worldly religious plans on the old Levitical patterns will not survive the wind and the waves, however skillful they are handled. The stirring of the Spirit in the hearts of ordinary believers and the truth of their call to be royal priests will shatter the chains that bound them to the pews and to the religious programs and buildings. The freedom of the Spirit will release the prisoners from the Levitical prison. They will walk out of the world of the church with its focus on earthly buildings, programs and structures to become living stones being built into a spiritual house to be a holy priesthood offering spiritual sacrifices acceptable to God through Jesus Christ. In time Levitical leaders will walk out too and as they do, they will break through the most critical wall of division in the body of Christ and discover the key to the unity that we need. It is time that we address the vital issue of unity that cannot be achieved as long as Levitical leadership exists in the church.

STEPPING ONTO THE ROAD OF UNITY

Our journey out of the world of the church opened our eyes to the key to unity in the body of Christ. As pastor of a local church I was always involved in the local ministerial fellowships. When we became more involved with prayer and prayer initiatives, the unity of the church became a central focus for us. We worked with many on different levels, attended conferences and seminars, taught, prayed whenever we could and with many from different backgrounds and worked for unity as much as we could. In the process we learned some very important lessons!

In the world of the church where unity is sought, doctrine (and tradition) and leadership are the focal points. When it comes to doctrine and tradition for example, evangelicals rarely join with liberals or Protestants with Catholics. Charismatics are a real challenge to non-charismatics, women in ministry a no-no for some, etc. Thus, whoever tries to get these groups together has his work cut out for him. **What they all do have in common is the basic leadership structure with its Levitical roots and the fact that Levitical leaders share common challenges in their work.** Therefore, in the world of the church it is commonly accepted that these leaders represent their local church and denomination. So, the first (and often only) step to expressing the unity of the church is to bring as many leaders together as possible with or without "lay representatives." This is not an easy task, for apart from the doctrinal and traditional divisions, one has to deal with individual personality issues. Add to that the schedules of these men and women who have expectations placed on them from different members in their respective churches all wanting individual attention from "the pastor whose salary they pay!" In this Levitical world interdenominational unity is just another program added to the many and depending on availability of time and a personal view of importance it will be placed on the priority list. For many leaders it is not a priority, for survival in the ministry with all its demands and the pressure of running the programs are more important.

Yet in the midst of these realities, in the church there is the growing sense of the importance of unity in the body of Christ. The Spirit of God is moving and those who seek him know there has to be more. It is very revealing that our Lord prayed about this just before he gave his life on the cross as we read in John 17:13-23: *I am coming to you now, but I* *say these things while I am still in the world, so that they may have the full measure of my joy within them. I have given them your word and the world has hated them, for they are not of this world any more than I am of this world. My prayer is not that you take them out of the world, but that you protect them from the evil one. They are not of this world, even as I am not of it. Sanctify them by the truth; your word is truth. As you sent me into the world, I have sent them into the world. For them I sanctify myself, so that they too may be sanctified. My prayer is not for them alone. I pray also for those who will believe in me through their message, that all of them may be one, Father, just as you are in me and I am in you. May they also be in us so that the world may believe that you have sent me. I have given them the glory that you gave me, so that they may be one as we are one: I in them and you in me. May they be brought to complete unity to let the world know that you sent me and have loved them even as you have loved me.*

Let us reflect on these words for a moment. First it is very clear that Jesus viewed the unity of the church as indispensable to be effective in sharing the gospel. Without unity the world will not believe the good news. Second, the church is not to be of this world. We are in the world, but should operate differently than the world. Now the very essence of what I tried to convey so far in this book is that the imposition of the Levitical system on the church by Constantine has undermined this very truth and the western church functions very much like a worldly corporation.[11] In fact, when we look at the serious attempts to bring unity to the divided body of Christ, we see this very clearly, for most seeking unity miss the fact that the church is an organism and not an institution. **The Levitical structure is the key problem to expressing and experiencing the unity of the body of Christ.** Let me illustrate this beginning with Psalm 133, which is very important to most that seriously wrestle with the unity issue:

How good and pleasant it is
when brothers live together in unity.
It is like the precious oil poured on the head,
running down on the beard,
running down on Aaron's beard,
down upon the collar of his robes.
It is as if the dew of Hermon
were falling on Mount Zion.
For there the Lord bestows his blessing,
even life forevermore.

The very essence of this Psalm is that it is steeped in the old covenant traditions. The anointing and subsequent blessing were tied to the Levitical high priest and the temple on Mount Zion. The unity of Israel that released the Lord's blessing depended upon the recognition

[11] This is why every church or ministry incorporates and with the tax incentives work to have charitable status. Having done this they are set up as corporations in accordance with the worldly system. Once we recognized that, we stepped away from it and we abandoned the ministry we founded and now simply work and minister without 'charitable status.'

of the Levitical leadership and submission to that leadership. This blessing and anointing flowed from the High Priest through the priestly temple ministry to the people underneath. **The problem is that the current Levitical church leadership in seeking unity does not recognize the old covenant roots in this Psalm. The lack of insight about the difference between the old covenant and the new leads to the assumption that the unity of the church is a matter of organization under Levitical headship. The fundamental issue that is not addressed is the fact that the greatest division in the body of Christ is that between clergy and laity. This is not addressed, because the only way the division can be overcome is by abolishing the current leadership model and accepting the order of Melchizedek, as we have stated many times.** We will return to this again, but first we have to further illustrate the point.

A while back one of the major initiatives to deal with roots of division in the Canadian church and with root issues affecting our nation was launched with a group touring from coast to coast. They made strategic stops on the way and local churches and believers joined in. We also attended when the group visited our area. It was a very well-planned event and prayerful discernment was evident, as many had sought the Lord in how to deal with the issues. Then at a very crucial stage during the event all "pastors and leaders" were called to come to the platform to participate and lead in the key prayers for healing divisions. I was immediately torn apart in my spirit. A part of me wanted to stay with the kingdom of priests that were forced to stand below the modern-day Levites looking down from the platform to do the "real ministry of reconciliation" on behalf of the people. The other part recognized that I was a leader and "invited" to step forward. Following the Spirit, I made my way up to the platform where I was led to quietly repent on behalf of the jubilant leaders who sought to bring unity while dividing the body of our Lord without even seeing it. As I stood on the platform and looked down I could sense the brokenness in the body so visibly displayed before my eyes and with that I sensed the grieving of the Spirit, even as excited leaders around me rejoiced being up there above the people to pray for unity while breaking it in the process! I wrestled with this for some time afterward and then wrote to one of the organizers whom I know personally and whom I respect (as I do the other leaders that were part of the initiative) sharing what I felt. I suggested that as they proceed across the country instead of dividing the body at that point, they simply invite everyone to share in the prayers. My suggestion was not followed and the individual has not only refused to acknowledge the receipt of the suggestion, but has avoided me since then. I have learned not to let such things bother me. **However, as I reflected on this later, I realized more than ever that we will never have true unity in the body of Christ until we address the root division between clergy and laity and turn**

away from the imposed Levitical model to the order of Melchizedek.

Allow me to share another example. Through many years I met with a local ministerial fellowship on a regular basis. I have seen this little group change from the customary ministerial to become caring and supportive more than anything else. However, it does represent the Levitical unity on the local level and is seen as such. Through the years various interdenominational unity events have been held. There has been one yearly event with a true effort to show forth the unity among the churches and that is the Easter sunrise service. While this was taking place the last time I attended I watched and again saw the same picture as above: This one event where we consciously tried to present the unity of the church had the people seated on the bleachers with the parade of pastors taking turns in the front – the body of the Lord cut in two while celebrating the resurrection of our Lord. Seeing this yet again, I wrestled with the issue of whether I should continue to meet with my friends in this way. On a personal level there is much benefit as the focus is on encouraging one another and praying and supporting one another. However, seen from the other side, the very unity which we seek can never come in this way and it is a waste of time and energy to think it brings unity to the divided body of the Lord. In fact, the key to unity is found in the passage so many of us see as foundational for the understanding of church leadership, but it is missed because we do not read it in the fuller context. So, let us read Ephesians 4 and note how unity and church leadership is linked.

As a prisoner for the Lord, then, I urge you to live a life worthy of the calling you have received. Be completely humble and gentle; be patient, bearing with one another in love. Make every effort to keep the unity in the Spirit through the bond of peace. There is one body and one Spirit – just as you were called to one hope when you were called – one Lord, one faith, one baptism, one God and Father of all, who is over all and through all and in all.

But to each one of us grace has been given as Christ apportioned it. This is why it says:

"When he ascended on high,
he led captives in his train
and gave gifts to men."

(What does "he ascended" mean except that he also descended to the lower earthly regions? He who descended is the very one who ascended higher than all the heavens, in order to fill the whole universe.) It was he who gave some to be apostles, some to be prophets, some to be evangelists and some to be pastors and teachers, to prepare God's people for the works of service, so that the body of Christ may be built up until we all reach unity in the faith and knowledge of the Son of God and become mature, attaining to the whole measure of the fullness of Christ.

Then we will no longer be infants, tossed back and forth by the waves, and blown here and there by every wind of teaching and by the cunning and craftiness of men in their deceitful scheming. Instead, speaking the truth in love, we will in all things grow up into him who is the Head, that is, Christ. From him the whole body, joined and held together by every supporting ligament, grows and builds itself up in love, as each part does its work.

The first thing to note is that the unity of the church is in the Spirit through the bond of peace. We were called to this unity which is in the Spirit. This is vital. The unity of the body of the Lord is neither in doctrine nor in organization. All of our efforts to bring forth unity by organizing events and running interdenominational programs are in vain. **Unity flows forth from being who we are in Christ and relating to other believers expressing his love through our actions, especially when we are being stretched and forced to be patient, gentle and humble.**

The second thing to note is that the task of the leaders is simply to equip the members of the body for their work of ministry. Implied in this is that once they are equipped, they are to be released to this work. As we have noticed in the previous chapter, in the early church the apostles simply made sure that the believers were filled with the Spirit and then they moved on. In the Spirit we have the full equipment we need for our work of ministry. It is through the Spirit that we are connected with the head, that is Christ, from whom we each get the direction for our ministry as royal priests.

As each member relates to Christ through the Spirit, the whole body functions in unity.

As we walked out of the world of the church our eyes were opened to see the unity of the body of our Lord in a very different way. Recognizing that leaders were called to equip the saints for the work of ministry and to release them, it was obvious that our unity will not be expressed through organizational means. It is in the Spirit. In fact, most in the church, including most leaders, do not understand the very nature of the church. In the western world we have been so blinded by our Levitical structures that we cannot see the inherent problem we face when it comes to expressing the unity of the church in these structures. **Rather than equip the saints for their work of ministry, leaders work to keep members in the local church, as supporters of the institution and for the income needed to maintain the church and pay staff salaries. The focus is on these 'needs' and little else. In terms of "equipping", it is a never-ending repetition of studies to keep people occupied and also to have them toe the party line, that is to make sure the people know what makes their local church different from the others. By keeping these walls of division strong, the people will not easily move to another church or out of the church. Much of the unity efforts are also political moves from the leaders to keep some order amidst the rivalries inherent in the**

denominational divisions, particularly as the religious pie of the community is only so big!

In the words of Ephesians 4 we actually face the reality that many in the institutional church are infants in the faith. They are driven by the teachings of men which brought about the denominational (and "independent" or non- denominational) bodies and some have been led astray by the cunning and craftiness of men in their deceitful scheming to be joined with the cults. Inherent in all the institutional organization of the church is the fact that the focus is first and foremost on the support and maintenance of the local church building, program and staff. This inevitably brings about and furthers division and rivalry between the local churches and their respective leaders. However, the infancy of the church's faith is most clearly visible in the fact that so few understand the true nature of the church and to this we need to look now.

The church is not an organization, but a living organism. The church is the body of Christ and its unity can only be understood as such. When Scripture speaks of the church as the body of the Lord, it is likened to a human body as we find for example in 1 Corinthians 12:12-27: *The body is a unit, though it is made up of many parts; and though all its parts are many, they form one body. So it is with Christ. For we were all baptized by one Spirit into one body – whether Jews or Greeks, slave or free – and we were all given the one Spirit to drink. Now the body is not made up of one part, but of many. If the foot should* *say, "Because I am not a hand, I do not belong to the body," it would not for that reason cease to be part of the body. And if the ear should say, "Because I am not an eye, I do not belong to the body," it would not for that reason cease to be part of the body. If the whole body were an eye, where would the sense of hearing be? If the whole body were an ear, where would the sense of smell be? But in fact, God has arranged the parts in the body, every one of them, just as he wanted them to be. If they were all one part, where would the body be? As it is, there are many parts, but one body. The eye cannot say to the hand, "I don't need you!" And the head cannot say to the feet, "I don't need you!" On the contrary, those parts that seem to be weaker are indispensable and the parts that we think are less honorable we treat with special honor. And the parts that are unpresentable we treat with special modesty, while our presentable parts need no special treatment. But God has combined the members of the body and has given greater honor to the parts that lacked it, so that there should be no division in the body, but that its parts should have equal concern for each other. If one part suffers, every part suffers with it; if one part is honored, every part rejoices with it. Now you are the body of Christ and each one of you is part of it.*

Now this passage is set into the larger context of the gifts of the Spirit and we will look at that later. However, the key points to note are clear. **First, the unity of the body is given.** Our actions do not bring about the unity! Our task is to express this unity in the way we relate to the other parts of the body! When we fail to express this (because we choose to do so), it does not alter the fact of the unity one iota, but it adversely affects the functioning of the body. **Second, the unity is in**

the Spirit. Thus, the effective expression of this unity flows from the way we listen and respond to the Spirit. This is why the setting of this passage is important, for the gifts of the Spirit are given to each member to minister to the needs of the other members – and this includes the leadership gifts in the church. **Third, there is to be equal concern for one another and no partiality.** In fact, this is why leadership is to be expressed by being servants modeling servant hood to the members of the body. The expression of our unity is vitally dependent on how we recognize and treat the least among us, that is those members of the body who seem to have nothing to offer! This is why the emphasis on those in positions of power ministering on the platform and in the front at the services is contrary to the very heart of the gospel. True leadership is not seen by the way we clothe or the way we operate in power, but by the way we build up each member and release him or her into the work of ministry. **Most importantly the body of Christ has one head and that is Christ Jesus himself.** He directs each member through the Spirit and our task is to submit to him and obey his Spirit. In doing this, the unity of the body is expressed and becomes visible to everyone.

When we walked out of the world of the church these truths became much more visible and real to us than when we were in the world of the church trying to encourage unity through getting together occasionally with others for this purpose. We were able to see that the unity of the church could not be expressed through the old covenant concepts. The denominations and groups meeting in church buildings under various names advertising their services on Sunday in the paper cannot be viewed as "the modern-day tribes" and the clergy and their leadership ruling like priests and Levites cannot bring unity by organizing interdenominational gatherings. Applying the basic lessons of the letter to the Hebrews that in Christ God replaced the Levitical model with the order of Melchizedek and *by calling this covenant "new," he made the first one obsolete,* we understood that the unity of the church will never be expressed in such ways. In fact, we need to apply these revelations to the very Scriptures we use from the old covenant to understand them correctly! Let me explain this by returning to Psalm 133 and let us seek the Spirit in this. It is vital that we live in unity and that our unity is expressed in a way that the world can see this. This unity is no longer found in the Levitical priesthood model with an earthly priest or leader like Aaron ministering on our behalf. It is found in the eternal High Priest Jesus Christ. Those who are joined to him in faith by being born again of water and the Spirit directly receive the anointing and the power of the Spirit from him as head and are transformed to be members of the body – even the least! The members of the body of Christ do not need another mediator or hierarchy of mediators between them and the head, Jesus, to transmit his anointing to them. Each one of these members is set free to move wherever the Spirit leads and to minister to other members in the Spirit. It has nothing to do with organizations and leaders running the show, but about obedience to the Spirit. In doing this God's blessing is released to every member directly through the Spirit and with it life forevermore.

As we walked out of the world of the church we walked not only into a new understanding of the unity of the church, but we walked into a freedom to express and live out this unity in a way that was not possible before. Today I simply listen to the Spirit and touch lives as he directs without worrying about the human boundaries that confine so many of God's people. We have become available to the Spirit in ways we could not be under the Levitical system. We do not seek confrontation with those bound by their traditions, just like the early believers who simply followed the Spirit's guidance. We truly seek to live in peace with all, but will not hesitate to minister to a need when directed by the Spirit. As we do this, we have seen people being set free from such human control and released to do the work of ministry to which they were called. Most of what we have learned has come in simple obedience to the Spirit and I thank God that he confined our ministry for an extended period to a very small group to teach us how to express unity in this way. At the same time, I was set free from the bondage of expectations that came with the old Levitical package of ministry! We do not try to please men and are not easily swayed by guilt trips when others expect us to do what they think we should. **It is much better to wait upon the Spirit than to fulfill man's expectations. God can do more in a split second through me**

if I respond to his Spirit than I can achieve in a lifetime of toil. The worldly model will get you to set a purpose and be driven to achieve that goal, and you may even win the world, but it is less effective than being still, while listening to the Spirit to hear his voice and direction, and simply follow in obedience.

With this, let us return again to the passage in 1 Corinthians 12 and the picture of the church as the body of Christ. This picture must also be understood in the light of the fact that the church in Corinth failed to express this unity as we read in the opening chapter, 1 Corinthians 1:10-17: *I appeal to you, brothers, in the name of our Lord Jesus Christ, that you agree with one another so that there may be no divisions among you and you may be perfectly united in mind and in thought. My brothers, some of Chloe's household have informed me that there are quarrels among you. What I mean is this: One of you says, "I follow Paul"; another, "I follow Apollos"; another, "I follow Cephas"; still another, "I follow Christ." Is Christ divided? Was Paul crucified for you? Were you baptized into the name of Paul? I am thankful that I did not baptize any of you except Crispus and Gaius, so that no one can say that they were baptized into my name. (Yes, I also baptized the household of Stephanas; beyond that I do not remember if I baptized anyone else.) For Christ did not send me to baptize, but to preach the gospel – not with words of human wisdom, lest the cross of Christ be emptied of its power.* This is followed later by the passage in 1 Corinthians 3 where Paul plainly stated that such divisions are from the world and not from the Spirit, e. g. 1 Corinthians 3:1-11: *Brothers, I could not address you as spiritual but as worldly – mere infants in Christ. I gave you milk, not solid food, for you were not ready for it. You are still worldly. For since there is jealousy and quarreling among you, are you not worldly? Are you not acting like mere men? For when one says, "I follow Paul," and another, "I follow Apollos," are you not mere men? What, after all, is Apollos? And what is Paul? Only servants through whom you came to believe – as the Lord had assigned to each his task. I planted the seed, Apollos watered it, but God made it grow. So neither he who plants nor he who waters is anything, but only God who makes things grow. The man who plants and the man who waters have one purpose, and each will be rewarded according to his own labor. For we are God's fellow workers; you are God's field, God's building. By the grace God has given me, I laid the foundation as an expert builder, and someone else is building on it. But each should be careful how he builds. For no one can lay any foundation other than the one already laid, which is Jesus Christ.* A little later in 1 Corinthians 3:16 Paul adds the following about the picture of the church as a building: *Don't you know that you yourselves are God's temple and that God's Spirit lives in you? If anyone destroys God's temple, God will destroy him; for God's temple is sacred, and you are that temple.*

In the same way Paul returned to the issue of unity in 1 Corinthians 11:17-34 when he addressed the divisions at the celebration of the Lord's supper. The words from 1 Corinthians 11:27-29 are most often quoted out of context by many in the church and refer to the unity of the body that is broken by our divisions: *Therefore, whoever eats the bread or drinks the cup of the Lord in an unworthy manner will be guilty of sinning against the body and blood of the Lord. A man ought to examine himself before he eats of the bread and drinks of the cup. For anyone who eats and drinks without recognizing the body of the Lord, eats and drinks judgment upon himself.* **In summary: The unity of the church is given and is rooted in the personal relationship of every member with Christ. This unity has to be expressed in all our interpersonal relationships in a way that visibly displays the love of Christ through our actions under the guidance of the Spirit.**

The picture of the church as the body of Christ in 1 Corinthians 12, which we quoted earlier, has to be seen against the background of the passages above. As I stand back and look at the world of the church displayed in print on the church page in the local newspaper, I do not see unity, but divisions similar to the ones Paul addressed in this letter. Many follow men and women in leadership. Some revere the dead leaders (Calvin, Knox, Wesley, etc.) and some flock to the current leaders, particularly those who are great speakers. Paul would have been appalled (Pun intended) to see many of today's churches bearing his name or the name of one of the other apostles and other church leaders. The way of worship and the programs are key selling points of the churches and thus we run our ads to attract our share of the customers. Competition can be fierce and it takes its toll on the clergy and their families. Leadership in the world of the church is not easy! Apart from the competition between the rival factions, there is also the delicate task to keep the local church's factions together, for little issues can quickly flare up to disrupt the peace and unity in that part of the body. **In the world of the church interdenominational meetings are the main ways that unity is expressed. These are carefully planned to ensure that local clergy in attendance are recognized and if possible, given a spot on the program. These meetings are few and far between and are rarely a key focus for the local churches as shown in the attendance of such functions. In addition to these meetings local ministerial meetings are held where clergy meet. Normally these meetings attract only a sample of the local clergy sharing similar broad theological views. At times these develop into fellowship groups where close friendships are made and support is given and truly show forth some aspects of the unity of the church through love and care in relationship.**

Again, as we walked out of the world of the church, we were able to see the picture from a very different view. **No matter how hard we tried, we could not fit the picture of the world of the church into the image of the body of Christ! No matter how hard we tried, the institutional model could not fit into the living organism we found in Scripture.** To this day I cannot see how any of the local churches meeting in a building called church with clergy and programs relate to the body. Is the Baptist church the arm? Is the Presbyterian church the leg? Are the clergy who all function like little heads a separate organ and if so, how do they relate to the rest and in particular to their local church? As I looked at the intentional efforts to express the unity of the church through occasional meetings, these efforts raised similar questions. What kind of body is this that has the arm, leg and some other parts function independently for 99% of the time and then randomly brings sample portions of these together in an institutional setting for a short time in order to 'proclaim unity' and then expect that 'unity' to bring forth a blessing from God and life forevermore? The reality of the church as represented by the institutional churches reminds one more of the rhetorical questions asked by Paul about the body parts that do not want to be connected to the other body parts.

More importantly is the division between clergy and laity. In the world of the church the clergy are generally seen as representatives of the churches. How does this fit with the concept of the body? I have never been represented by any part of my body! It just does not work. In the body there is no such option and the division of the body in this manner is the most fundamental division in the church. This raises the issue of the celebration of the Lord's supper. In the Roman Catholic tradition, the sacraments are strictly to be administered by the clergy and this tradition has for the most part been followed in the Protestant churches, except that we have reduced these to baptism and the celebration of the Lord's supper. There is not a shred of Biblical support for a need for clergy to administer baptism or the Lord's supper, but it is widely practiced. **This leads to the fact that in most churches every time the Lord's supper is celebrated the body of the Lord is not recognized as the unity is visibly broken. This means that most churches eat and drink in judgment upon themselves as they tolerate and practice this unholy division of the Lord's people into clergy and laity.**

The concept of the church as body cannot be expressed through any institutional structures. The church can only function on the basis of relationship. It is not an organization to which we belong, but a living organism of which we are all part. One cannot organize organic life! The church's unity flows from the relationship with Christ, which brings forth the life that sets the rest in place and in relationship, as Jesus said in John 15. We will look at this shortly, but first have to deal with another concept that is nothing more than human organization in the world of the church to make relationship happen within the church – the "cell church structure."

On the surface the "cell church" seems to fit with the Biblical concept of the church as the body of Christ. It seems to apply the scientific truth of cells to the Biblical concept. However, the Biblical picture never referred to cells, but to parts of the body like arms, eyes, legs, etc. In other words, even though it looks like an application of Scripture, it is reading into the text concepts that are foreign to the context. More importantly though, the way most cell churches operate reveal the worldly model being used. This model is nothing else than the Multi-Level Marketing pyramids clothed in religious verbiage. As in the business world, this model when pushed certainly works to build an organization, and churches that apply these concepts build some of the most successful Levitical kingdoms. However, the key issue is that the focus is on the local church as Levitical kingdom represented by the pyramid needing an ever-broadening base to raise the top leadership higher! The leaders above them in the pyramid control the "cells" in this body and the authority is centralized in the top leadership. **The very structure is precisely the opposite of the servant leadership that Jesus modeled and taught, where the leaders serve the people and kneel to wash their feet, rather than oversee from the top of the pyramid!**

These matters became much clearer to us as we found ourselves outside the Levitical structures in which we had worked and ministered for many years. Moving out of these structures I never consciously thought about some of these issues, but as I reflected upon our journey, I was able to see the church in a new light. **It became very obvious that the unity of the church is inherently given and the problem we face is how to express that. Further, it became even more obvious that this given unity cannot be expressed through organizing events and programs and least of all without addressing the very basic division between clergy and laity**

inherent in the Levitical systems. However, when we read the New Testament it is clear that unity is in the Spirit and naturally flows from our relationship in Christ expressed in the way we follow the Spirit to serve one another, as we read in John 15:1-17.

I am the true vine and my Father is the gardener. He cuts off every branch in me that bears no fruit, while every branch that does bear fruit, he prunes so that it will be even more fruitful. You are already clean because of the word I have spoken to you. Remain in me and I will remain in you. No branch can bear fruit by itself; it must remain in the vine. Neither can you bear fruit unless you remain in me. I am the vine; you are the branches. If a man remains in me and I in him, he will bear much fruit. Apart from me you can do nothing. If anyone does not remain in me, he is like a branch that is thrown away and withers; such branches are picked up, thrown into the fire and burned. If you remain in me and my words remain in you, ask whatever you wish and it will be given to you. This is to my Father's glory, that you bear much fruit, showing yourselves to be my disciples. As the Father has loved me, so have I loved you. Now remain in my love. If you obey my commands, you will remain in my love, just as I have obeyed the Father's commands and remain in his love. I have told you this so that my joy may be in you and your joy may be complete. My command is this: Love each other as I have loved you. Greater love has no one than this, that he lay down his life for his friends. You are my friends if you do what I command. I no longer call you servants, because a servant does not know his master's business. Instead, I have called you friends, for everything that I learned from my Father I have made known to you. You did not choose me, but I chose you and appointed you to go and bear fruit – fruit that will last. Then the Father will give you whatever you ask in my name. This is my command: Love each other.

These words speak for themselves and are not difficult to understand. **The unity of the church is found in the relationship with the Lord and it is expressed as we love one another with a willingness to lay down our lives for one another. This unity transcends all human barriers through the Spirit.** This is why we read in 1 Corinthians 12:12-13 that *the body is a unit, though it is made up of many parts; and though all its parts are many, they form one body. For we were all baptized by one Spirit into one body – whether Jews or Greeks, slave or free – and we were all given the same Spirit to drink.* In the same way we read in Galatians 3:26-29: *You are all sons of God through faith in Christ Jesus, for all of you who were baptized into Christ have clothed yourselves with Christ. There is neither Jew nor Greek, slave nor free, male nor female, for you are all one in Christ Jesus. If you belong to Christ, then you are Abraham's seed, and heirs according to the promise.* Then we read Galatians 4:4-7, *but when the time had fully come, God sent his Son, born of a woman, born under the law, to redeem those under the law, that we might receive the full rights of sons. Because you are sons, God sent the Spirit of his Son into our hearts, the Spirit who calls out, "Abba, Father." So you are no longer a slave, but a son; and since you are a son, God made you also an heir.*

Let us tie these things together. **The unity of the body of our Lord is given as a reality in the Spirit. Those who have been born again, that** means those who are baptized by water and the Spirit, are members of this one body as we have seen repeatedly in the Scriptures above. Our task is simply to express this unity in the way that we submit to the Lord and serve one another as the Spirit directs. It has absolutely nothing to do with organizational models, but with relationships. Therefore, those called to leadership are not to build organizations, but to equip the members for their work of ministering to the other members. The ministry of leaders is by nature itinerant and not settled, moving as the Spirit directs and where he opens the doors. Leaders do not own any part of the body and are to work together, crossing paths as they minister where the Spirit takes them. The ultimate goal is for every member to be fully equipped and released to be all he or she has been ordained to be by our Lord, firmly tied to him as head and led by the Spirit. It is about Jesus and each member's relationship with him through the Spirit. The unity is expressed as each member hears the voice of the Spirit and responds in obedience to serve others expressing the love of Christ to one another. It flows as natural as the functions of our human bodies. There are no boundaries to this expression of God's love through us and as we each respond to the Spirit, the barriers are broken down and the

expression of unity becomes more obvious and more effective.

As I observed earlier, these truths really only became revealed to me as I looked back on our journey out of the world of the church. When we were inside the world of the church, we were too busy trying to bring about unity through events and meetings with "key leaders and intercessors" and missed the very point. Yes, we taught and preached about the church as the body of Christ and unity issues, but we failed to see that reality of the body of Christ because we never experienced body life! By God's grace we were joined with a few friends and learned to function as members of the body without the baggage of the Institutional church. At the same time God called us to walk the extra mile and beyond that with others to bring one lost sheep back into the fold, one member of his body that is dislocated and hurting. As we obeyed the Lord the price became much higher than we ever imagined as I shared earlier in the book. We were literally asked to lay all we had on the line for one member that we had never met and would only meet in person near the end of our journey through the wilderness. In the process of helping this one man we walked into such lack of resources that we had no choice but to stay in a very confined social circle. The little house church and a few others became a part of the crucible in which we were refined to experience body life. However, in this process we also learned to trust the Spirit to guide each member individually and also corporately when gathered with other members. As this happened, we became aware of the truths shared above and that the unity in Christ Jesus flows out of each member's submission to the leading of the Spirit. **True body life opened our eyes to the fact that unity flows forth from our relationship with Christ as simple and as natural as a branch bears fruit when tied to the vine. When we took our hands off and trusted the Spirit instead of trying to run a program, lives blossomed. As we served as leaders by building others up without expecting them to serve our agenda, the reality of the order of Melchizedek was revealed and ordinary people became extraordinary royal priests. Instead of trying to make unity happen, it just came naturally in the Spirit as we served one another.**

What we saw and experienced on a small scale on our journey was confirmed in my spirit when someone recently gave us the book "The heavenly man" by Paul Hattaway. This book is the story of a leader in the house churches in China and it reads like a modern-day Book of Acts. In this book it is remarkable to find the unity in the church body and how it flowed naturally through the Spirit. **That unity was broken only when western churches added their theological books to shipments of Bibles, thereby introducing the divisive denominational doctrines to the house churches. It was restored as the Chinese leaders made a conscious choice to focus on Christ and the unity in the Spirit and when they**

returned to simply being the church! It is very interesting to read the observations of brother Yun when he finally came to the west and saw the western church in all its Levitical order. It is even more interesting to read about the Chinese church's missionaries being sent out and their focus and training. However, to return to the issue of the church's unity, this book confirmed to me that we will never get unity through current endeavors in the western churches until we deal with the root issues and move out of the Levitical structure. **The fundamental choice is between the church as organization or as living organism. In this there is no compromise possible. At the heart of the matter is the question whether or not we trust the Spirit to guide the church – on the individual as well as the corporate levels. The unity of the church is given and it becomes visibly expressed where each member responds to the leading of the Spirit in submission to the Lord, the head of the body. This is a spiritual truth that can only be understood by revelation. Once understood, it takes one out of the world of organization into true relationship that transcends all human boundaries with a willingness to serve others in every way that the Spirit directs.**

We can also look at this from another angle to see this in perspective: If I were to occasionally take a sample of some of my body parts, for example a little piece of liver, heart, a hair, piece of toe nail, etc. and put it in a container on display, would anyone recognize the collection as "Willie Joubert?" Moreover, will these samples of body parts function as the living being that I am? It is ridiculous to even think about it, yet this is precisely what our efforts to express the unity of the church by bringing together some "representatives" of various church groups once in a while accomplish. The church is an organic whole and every part is interconnected and serves a particular function. Occasionally some parts physically come together according to the needs to be served, as my hands serve to wash my feet at times. However, some parts serve other parts without ever physically touching, as my heart serves the same feet to meet a different need by pumping blood to them. **All of these things happen as the Lord directs according to his plan and purpose for the human body! Likewise, with the body of our Lord, most of what happens is not through conscious human planning, but through the Spirit in whom we have unity. As one little person touches a neighbor in need, the body is served. As itinerant leaders move around and touch lives and move on, like the blood flowing through our bodies, the various parts are served with encouragement and built up in faith. In everything, the Lord as the head of the body directs each part through the Spirit. The unity becomes visible as each little person touches other lives expressing the love of Christ in service to build others up in faith and service. This cannot be organized and managed in any way! It is by the Spirit who is like the wind and**

those who are born again move and minister in divine unity as he directs.

Earlier we looked at our Lord's prayer before he went to the cross, recorded in John 17. As we noted our Lord prayed specifically for those who believed in him and those who would in generations to come believe in him. **More importantly, he prayed that we as believers would be one as he is one with the Father, so that the world may know that the Father sent him.** It is vitally important to grasp this in the context of this prayer. In Christ we have been born again or in the words of Paul in 2 Corinthians 5:17-20, *"Therefore, if anyone is in Christ, he is a new creation; the old has gone, the new has come! All of this is from God, who reconciled us to himself in Christ and gave us the ministry of reconciliation: that God was reconciling the world to himself in Christ, not counting men's sins against them. And he has committed to us the message of reconciliation. We are therefore Christ's ambassadors, as though God was making his appeal through us. We implore you on Christ's behalf: Be reconciled to God!"* Now, in the words of our Lord, even though we are still in the world, **we are not of the world any more than Jesus is of the world.** By grace we have been changed and as we walk in unity with the Father and our Lord and with one another, his presence in us shows forth the glory of God. We are indeed *a chosen people, a royal priesthood, a holy nation, a people belonging to God, that we may declare the praises of him who called us out of darkness into his marvelous light,* as we read in 1 Peter 2:9. Having been chosen by God we are sent into the world as Jesus was sent into the world by the Father. This is why he prayed this prayer for us! **However, we were called out of darkness – but are in this world!** We were called out of darkness and into his marvelous light to become the light of the world. His glory is to shine forth in the darkness of the world as we express the unity of his body in the way we relate to one another in the love that knows no boundaries.

Here is the issue: We were called to function as the body of Christ in the world in the unity of the Spirit. In doing this we serve one another and display the power of his reconciling love to a world in desperate need of that love. The early church did this and amidst persecution and suffering the glory of God spread through ordinary people as they walked in the freedom and the unity of the Spirit. However, in time the structure of the church was changed and it became a worldly religious institution that eventually spawned many varieties of "churches." This brought many divisions to the body, most notably denominational and between clergy and laity and with these competition, persecution, religious wars, control, abuse and much more. Instead of being the people of God in the world, the church brought the world and its darkness into the church and made it into an increasing number of religious institutions battling one another. Unable to display a credible unity, the church in the western world has lost its power and

does not make a difference to our society. The divisions within the church have brought about walls that are very difficult to break down, thus hurting the credibility of our message. Even worse, the focus on church buildings in which the religious meet and run the programs, effectively built walls between the church and the world. The light of the world is now being covered under the steeples and roofs of the world of the church and the world in need of this light is kept in darkness. The answer is not to try to express a superficial unity by bringing representatives from different institutional churches together from time to time for a joint service or program. The only way to unity is to walk out of the world of the church and shed the institutional baggage to be the church in the world. There is a price to be paid as one walks through the gate into the wilderness, but we were called to be a pilgrim people, sent into the world.

THE DESERT SHALL BLOOM

As I wrote in the beginning, we stepped out of the world of the church and began a journey of learning and discovery that opened our eyes to see as we have never seen before. Having observed with new eyes, I began writing this book for those who are tired of the world of the church and all that it entails, but like us are passionate about the Lord and willing to walk in a radical authenticity following the Spirit wherever he may lead them. In this I wanted to share some of our journey and some of the things that we experienced. Moreover, I wanted to share some of the adjustments we had to make in the way we looked at the church, in order that the readers may on the one hand be encouraged in their journey and on the other hand may avoid pitfalls that will lead them back into the very bondage they wanted to escape. It is not just about a new paradigm of living. There is a price to be paid by all that walk out of the world of the church to follow the Spirit and walk in the freedom of the Spirit.

It is a journey into the wilderness of the world and many who walk through the gates of Levitical control into the freedom of the Spirit soon begin to look back to the old comfort zone, not unlike the Israelites who crossed the Red Sea and yet were quickly ready to return to bondage because they missed the food of Egypt! It is vital to understand this, for without seeing the journey in perspective, many miss their call and purpose on this earth. The perspective we need is found in many places in Scripture and we begin with two very short parables recorded in Matthew 13:44-46: *The kingdom of heaven is like a treasure hidden in a field. When a man found it, he hid it again. Then in his joy he went and sold all he had and bought that field. Again, the kingdom of heaven is like a merchant looking for fine pearls. When he found one of great value, he went away and sold everything he had and bought it.*

The pursuit of the kingdom of God will cost you everything! It is worth it, but it will cost you everything. It is the way of the cross and it is the only way to true freedom. In talking about the cost of being a disciple Jesus said the following as we read in Luke 14:26-33: *If anyone comes to me and does not hate his father and his mother, his wife and his children, his brothers and his sisters – yes, even his own life – he cannot be my disciple. And anyone who does not carry his own cross and follow me cannot be my disciple. Suppose one of you wants to build a tower. Will he not first sit down and estimate the cost to see if he has enough money to complete it? For if he lays the foundation and is not able to finish it, everyone who sees it will ridicule him, saying, "This fellow began to build, but was not able to finish." Or suppose a* *king is about to go to war against another king. Will he not first sit down and consider whether he is able with ten thousand men to oppose the one coming against him with twenty thousand? If he is not able, he will send a delegation while the other is still a long way off and will ask for terms of peace. In the same way, any of you who does not give up everything he has, cannot be my disciple.*

When we consider the message of these passages of Scripture, it is simple: The kingdom of God is worth pursuing, but it will cost everything we have! The kingdom of God calls for a radical authentic life of obedience to the Spirit in following Jesus and becoming like him. In the words of Philippians 2:5-11, *your attitude should be the same as Christ Jesus:*

Who, being in the very nature of God,
did not consider equality with God something to be grasped,
but made himself nothing,
taking the very nature of a servant, being made in human likeness.
And being found in the appearance as a man, he humbled himself,
and became obedient to death – even death on a cross.
Therefore God exalted him to the highest place,
and gave him a name that is above every name,
that at the name of Jesus every knee should bow,
in heaven and on earth and under the earth,
and every tongue shall confess that Jesus Christ is Lord,
to the glory of the Father

Here is the issue we need to consider: It is about being disciples and following Jesus Christ. In this most of us, having had our mindsets shaped by the religious world of the church, face similar issues as the early Jewish believers faced when the gospel spread and Gentiles came to faith. The religious and cultural baggage clouded their mindsets, especially when it came to the issues of circumcision, dietary laws and the Levitical order, as we know from the Book of Acts, Paul's letter to the Galatians and the letter to the Hebrews. As I have illustrated repeatedly throughout this book, the world of the church is nothing else than the old Levitical order, though abolished in Christ, having been resurrected under Constantine by sprinkling it with a mix of worldly wisdom and religious ideas in the name of Jesus. In the process, rather than being in the world but not of the world, the church moved out of the world and built walls to separate 'the believers' from the world. Yet at the same time it took much of the world dressed in religious garb inside into the walls of the church to create 'the world of the church.' This was done 'in the name of Jesus,' but is absolutely contrary to the person and message of our Lord. The only way out of this is graphically illustrated in Hebrews 13:11-14: *The high priest carries the blood of animals into the Most Holy Place as a sin offering, but the bodies are burned outside the camp. And so Jesus also suffered outside the city gate to make his people holy through his own blood. Let us, then, go to him outside the camp, bearing the disgrace he bore. For here we do not have an enduring city, but we are looking for the city that is to come.*

The church is called to follow Jesus and the direction of its ministry is away from the Levitical structures of the Old Covenant. In the letter to the Hebrews the earthly Jerusalem embodies the Old Levitical structure which was made obsolete by the new order of Melchizedek when Jesus was rejected and crucified outside the gate. The city gate represents the place of judgment and control. The religious leaders and the people rejected Jesus Christ and he was taken outside the city gate where he suffered and died on the cross. He is the stone that the builders rejected and became the capstone of the new temple, built not with stone and mortar and not by human hands. We are likewise to follow him as disciples through the gates of Levitical control outside the religious structures and go into the world with a willingness to be rejected and to suffer and give our lives for the sake of the Kingdom. Ours is a call into the wilderness of the world and not a flight out of the world to hide behind sacred walls. We are called to journey to a city that is to come from heaven, not to build and to manage earthly structures that we call sanctuaries or churches. It is the walk of faith, *being sure of what we hope for and certain of what we do not see* (Hebrews 11:1). In this we are encouraged by the heroes of faith and what they did and how they endured suffering, rejection and much more as summarized in Hebrews 11:4-38 after which we read verses 39-40: *These were all commended for their faith, yet none of them received what had been promised. God had planned something better for us so that only together with us would they be made perfect.* Their faith is tied together with ours into a glorious unity that will be perfected as we walk out of the confinement of the worldly religious structures, moved by the Spirit wherever we are needed for the Kingdom.

This is the way of the cross, which is the power of the God released in and through us. Thus we are encouraged in the words of Hebrews 12:1-4: *Therefore, since we are surrounded by such a great cloud of witnesses, let us throw off everything that hinders and the sin that so easily entangles, and let us run with perseverance the race marked out for us. Let us fix our eyes on Jesus, the author and perfecter of our faith, who for the joy set before him endured the cross, scorning its shame, and sat down at the right hand of God. Consider him who endured so much opposition from sinful men, so that you will not grow weary and loose heart. In your struggle against sin, you have not yet resisted to the point of shedding your blood.* As I have stated in many ways, the key issue that hinders most western believers in this race is the traditional paradigm of the church being viewed and expressed in organizational terms. Like the Pharisees we have nullified the word of God with our traditions and we need to throw these away and walk out into the world to be the church we are called to be. **The heart of our faith is in Christ who was sent to this world and then sent us into the wilderness of this world through which we travel to a city that is not of this world, the heavenly Jerusalem.** To get this in perspective we simply have to listen to the Scriptures in order to grasp that we are apostolic (sent) people and I challenge you to listen to the Spirit as you read the following:

John 3:16-17: *For <u>God so loved the world that he gave his one and only Son,</u> so that whoever believes in him shall not perish, but have everlasting life. <u>For God did not sent his Son into the</u>*

world to condemn the world, but to save the world through him. These words were spoken to Nicodemus when he visited Jesus at night and they follow the words of Jesus that no one could see the Kingdom unless he is born again, that means moving and acting by the Spirit. In John 20:21-23 the resurrected Lord appears to the disciples and says: *"Peace be with you. As the Father has sent me, I am sending you." With that he breathed on them and said: "Receive the Holy Spirit."* Our mission is a mission in and to the world. Like Jesus we are called to share the love of God with the world in which we live and to this end we have received the Spirit and the divine power to do the work. However, it comes with a price and that is obedience to move and minister wherever the Spirit leads and a willingness to give all that has been entrusted to us, including our lives. This is clearly illustrated in the passages of Scripture where our Lord sent his disciples forth. So, let us look at these and again let the Spirit speak to you as you read these Scriptures.

The first time Jesus sent his disciples out, it followed a particular instance in his ministry as we read in Matthew 9:35-10:1: *Jesus went through all the towns and villages, teaching in their synagogues, preaching the good news of the kingdom and healing every disease and sickness. When he saw the crowds, he had compassion on them, because they were harassed and helpless, like sheep without a shepherd. Then he said to his disciples, "The harvest is plentiful but the workers are few. Ask the Lord of the harvest, therefore, to send out workers into his harvest field." He called his twelve disciples to him and gave them authority to drive out evil spirits and to heal every disease and sickness.* The key issue to note here is that the mission was in response to Jesus' compassion on the people and the need in the world. Following this we find the instructions given to the disciples on this occasion and some of the things they could expect, as we read the following selections from Matthew 10:5-42: *Do not go among the Gentiles or enter any town of the Samaritans. Go rather to the lost sheep of Israel. As you go, preach this message: "The kingdom of heaven is near." Heal the sick, raise the dead, cleanse those who have leprosy, drive out demons. Freely you have received freely give. Do not take along any gold or silver or copper in your belts; take no bag for the journey, or extra tunic, or sandals or a staff; for the worker is worth his keep (5-10). I am sending you out like sheep among wolves. Therefore, be shrewd as snakes and as innocent as doves. Be on guard against men; they will hand you over to the local councils and flog you in their synagogues. On my account you will be brought before governors and kings as witnesses to them and to the Gentiles (16-18). Do not be afraid of them. There is nothing concealed that will not be disclosed, or hidden that will not be made known. Do not be afraid of those who kill the body but cannot kill the soul. Rather, be afraid of the One who can destroy both soul and body in hell. Are not two sparrows sold for a penny? Yet not one of them will fall to the ground apart from the will of your Father. And even the very hairs of your head are numbered. So, don't be afraid; you are worth more than many sparrows (26, 28-31). Anyone who does not take up his cross and follow me is not worthy of me. Whoever finds his life will lose it, and whoever loses his life for my sake will find it (38-39).*

Now, before we look at these words, it is important to note that Luke recorded the sending out of the twelve in a shorter form in chapter 9. In addition to this he also recorded a subsequent sending out of 72 other disciples in strikingly similar terms than what we have read in Matthew. This is found in Luke 10 and begins with the same concern about the harvest that is plentiful, but the workers few. There are some key differences that we need to see, though: First the fact that this was not only a bigger group, but we have no names to identify any. Second, the mission was no longer restricted to only "the lost sheep of Israel." Third, following this mission we read in Luke 10:17-24: *The seventy-two returned with joy and said: "Lord, even the demons submit to us in your name!" He replied: "I saw Satan fall like lightning from heaven. I have given you authority to trample on snakes and scorpions and to overcome all the power of the enemy; nothing will harm you. However, do not rejoice that the spirits submit to you, but rejoice that your names are written in heaven."*

At that time Jesus, full of joy through the Holy Spirit, said: "I praise you, Father, Lord of heaven and earth, because you have hidden these things from the wise and learned, and revealed them to little children. Yes, Father, that was for your good pleasure. No one knows who the Son is except the Father, and no one knows who the Father is except the Son and those to whom the Son chooses to reveal him." Then he turned to his disciples and said privately, "Blessed are the eyes that see what you see. For I tell you that many prophets and kings wanted to see what you see but did not see it, and to hear what you hear but did not hear it."

As we walked out of the world of the church, like Jesus we found many of God's people outside the walls of the church. It is here that we truly began to understand the compassion of our Lord for those in need, for they are indeed wandering the hills like sheep without a shepherd. In fact, there are more Christians outside the church walls than inside! This holds true not only for nominal Christians that moved out of the liberal institutional churches, but also for "born again believers" who left their evangelical churches and "Spirit filled Christians" who left the Charismatic and independent Charismatic churches. **Those inside the walls lament "the loss of members" which at times causes some churches to close the doors. Some therefore try with worldly wisdom and worldly methods covered in religious terminology to draw them back into the walls.** Thus, we find the "programs of outreach and evangelism" and the "seeker sensitive methods," etc. to get "the back sliders" back into the church. Some return, often to be hurt and leave again. However, many do not return and contrary to what some believe, not all are "back sliders!" There are many that are deeply committed to the Lord and seek the Kingdom and its righteousness. They have moved through the gates into the wilderness of the world and have rejected the institutional church paradigm. Many of these are hurting and wandering the hills like sheep without a shepherd, but they have not rejected the Lord. More than that, many have left because the Lord cared so much for them that he would not let them stay imprisoned in the four walls with its Levitical leadership and programs. **Having said this, I believe there is a prophetic message for the church in the**

passages above: Just like the mission of Jesus started in the synagogues and moved out into the world, beginning with the Jews and then moved beyond to the Samaritans and Gentiles, so are we being directed outwards by the Spirit. We experienced this personally. After we had moved through the gates of religious control into the world, we found many hurting and wounded believers, just like Jesus found. As we saw them, we were filled with compassion for them and began to minister to them. Soon we noticed that the task was enormous, as there is such a great harvest. There are many workers needed and we pray and ask the Lord of the harvest to send more workers.

The deeply committed believers outside the walls of the church are the most readily available workers, but they often need healing and they need to experience the reality of the church as presented in the New Testament to replace the old paradigm which they rejected. I sense in the Spirit that the Lord has been preparing servant leaders currently being sent into our communities, like the twelve, to minister first and foremost to the hurting believers outside the walls of the Institutional Churches. As we ourselves moved outside the walls of the church, we met other leaders who share the same vision to see the restoration of the church as we read in the pages of the New Testament and like us, they have rejected the unscriptural paradigm of the church as institution. These servants are being sent forth to minister as servants and to learn to be servants and to trust the Father (not the church) for provision. They cooperate with one another, however not in a formal sense, but simply as brothers and sisters in the Lord, seeking to further the Kingdom. They do not plant and build traditional institutional churches, but simply minister as the Spirit leads, bringing healing and restoration to the body of Christ. In the process the Spirit sets up key divine appointments and prepares specific homes to become Kingdom centers in the community.[12] **As a result many anointed new leaders are being equipped (and will be equipped) by the servant leaders, while homes are opened as Kingdom ministry centers. These new leaders will become a second and bigger group of workers that will go forth like the seventy-two disciples sent forth by the Lord to reach yet more in the world, including those who are nominal believers and many who do not know the Lord at all.**

Just like the seventy-two sent forth by Jesus, the second wave of workers will be no-names, unknown and unrecognized by many, but known and anointed by the Lord. Walking in the Spirit and acting in simple faith and obedience, they will be a powerful witness in the

[12] It is important to note that when Jesus sent his disciples on the first missions he told them to find "a man of peace" in the cities they enter and make this person's home the base of the ministry (Matthew 10:11-13 and Luke 10:5-7). Today this strategy is followed with great success in many parts of the world.

world. Ordinary people understanding who they are in Christ will be extraordinary royal priests in the order of Melchizedek and will walk in a powerful anointing. They will be mighty instruments in the hand of our Lord to transform local communities and even nations. We can testify to the power and anointing released as ordinary people are set free to do the work of ministry. It is not about religious studies, degrees earned at seminaries, credentials or even organizational methods. As Jesus said, the Father reveals the hidden things to those who simply believe like children. The simple faith exercised in obedience to the words of our Lord and to the guidance of the Spirit brings forth amazing results and even dislodge Satan from his strongholds in our communities. This ties in with the words of our risen Lord given to the disciples before he ascended into heaven, so let us look at these now. We begin with Mark 16:15-18: *He said to them: "Go into all the world and preach the good news to all creation. Whoever believes and is baptized will be saved, but whoever does not believe will be condemned. And these signs will accompany those who believe: In my name they will drive out demons; they will speak in new tongues; they will pick up snakes with their hands; and when they drink deadly poison, it will not hurt them at all; they will place their hands on sick people and they will get well."*

It is important to note what is said and what is not said! First, Jesus did not command us to build buildings, run programs, set up seminaries and train clergy who are to be paid to run the church! The ministry is entrusted

to all that believe and as they exercise this, they can expect to see captives set free and miraculous healing. There is nothing about "laity" being helpers to maintain buildings, teach programs, clean the church, fold bulletins, greet people at the door, and attend meetings and endless Bible Studies. Second, we are sent forth into the world and not to build walls to isolate the believers from the world and create "Kingdom clubs for members only!" Our mission is to go into the world to share the message of God's love to the world and reach out in compassion to meet the needs of people. Matthew 28:18-20 reads: *Then Jesus came to them and said: "All authority in heaven and on earth has been given to me. Therefore, go and make disciples of all nations, baptizing them in the name of the Father and of the Son and of the Holy Spirit. Teach them to obey everything I have commanded you. And surely, I am with you always, to the very end of the age."* Again, it is important to note what is said and what not. We note the same as in Mark 16:15-18 above. The mission is into the world to make disciples and to teach them to obey everything the Lord commanded. This has nothing to do with setting up organizations and getting people involved in supporting these! It is about living in relationship with the risen Lord, sharing the love of God in word and in deed as we move into the world in obedience to where the Spirit may lead us.

It is no surprise that the same message is found in the Book of Acts. The stage was set for the mission and ministry of the church by the risen Lord prior to his ascension as recorded in chapter 1:4-8: *On one occasion, while he was eating with them, Jesus gave them this command: "Do not leave Jerusalem, but wait for the gift my Father promised, which you have heard me speak about. For John baptized with water, but in a few days, you will be baptized with the Holy Spirit." So, when they met together, they asked him: "Lord, are you at this time going to restore the kingdom to Israel?" He said to them: "It is not for you to know the times or dates the Father has set by his own authority. But you will receive power when the Holy Spirit comes upon you; and you will be my witnesses in Jerusalem, and in all of Judea and Samaria, and to the ends of the earth." After he said this, he was taken up before their very eyes, and a cloud hid him from their sight.* Again, it is not difficult to understand these words. Equipped by the Spirit the believers were sent out, beginning where they were and commanded to go out to the ends of the earth. It is important to note that the first disciples were Jewish and even in the presence of the risen Lord they were still thinking first about the kingdom of Israel, equating that with the Kingdom of God. Even though our Lord expressly repeated that their mission is outwards and away from their Jewish comfort zone, these disciples struggled with the religious baggage of the old Levitical covenant. They remained 'Jerusalem focused' and tied to the temple in many ways. It was not until, after the stoning of Stephen spilled over in persecution, that they moved out and away from Jerusalem into Samaria and beyond. As this happened God opened Peter's eyes through a vision to open the door for Gentiles with the conversion of Cornelius and after that others moved beyond the Jewish comfort zones in Antioch. Finally, God cut the ties with Jerusalem and the temple when the Romans destroyed it in AD 70. **In my opinion this is also a prophetic sign for the church of our day. As believers begin to truly move in the Spirit in obedience, they will move beyond the walls of the current Levitical paradigm and it will bring forth religious persecution from those who have a vested interest in the preservation of the Institutional Church.** There are many that are no different from the disciples in Acts 1, except they equate the Institutional Church (especially their chosen denomination) with the Kingdom of God. They have a hard time seeing and hearing what the Spirit is saying to the church, because they think about church in organizational terms and are as inwardly looking 'church and building focused' as the early disciples were 'Jerusalem and temple focused.' Questioning that paradigm is viewed as attacking the church, and from that perspective those who follow the wind of the Spirit are viewed mostly in a negative light. **However, the Spirit is moving and restoring the church to be the church in the world. Like the days of Acts God will use persecution and rejection (and if needed the destruction of the Institutional Church) to propel believers out of the walls to be his peculiar people and witnesses in the wilderness of the world. We are called and sent forth into the world as ambassadors of the Kingdom of heaven.**

Ultimately it is a matter of where our focus is and where we invest out lives. In the Sermon on the mount Jesus said it in these words in Matthew 6:19-21: *Do not store up for yourselves treasures on earth, where moth and rust destroy, and thieves break in and steal. Rather, store up for yourselves treasures in heaven, where moth and rust do not destroy and where thieves do not break in and steal. For where your treasure is, there will your heart be also.* For years we have been sold the story that the pursuit of the Kingdom of God is to be involved in and invest in the Institutional Church with its buildings, programs and structures. Many of us have worked and got tired to keep old buildings up and keep the doors open, in the mistaken belief that God is somehow dependent on these buildings and programs to meet his people. In very real terms I have pastored churches where we struggled with the maintenance and upkeep of buildings, for 'moth and rust and decay' caused major repair needs and we literally dealt with thieves breaking in and stealing! However, we were so blinded by the institutional model of the church, we saw this as essential to the Kingdom of God and sadly our focus caused us to invest in these earthly treasures! In the words of Hebrews 12:1-2 and 13:12-14 we are commanded to *throw off everything that hinders and the sin that so easily entangles and run the race marked out for us with perseverance. Let us fix our eyes (focus) on Jesus, the author and perfecter of our faith, who for the joy set before him endured the cross, scorning its shame, and sat down at the right hand of God. He suffered outside the city gate to make the people holy through his own blood. Let us, then, go to him outside the camp, bearing the disgrace he bore. For here we do not have an enduring city, but we are looking for the city that is to come.*

Our call is to go into the world and into the wilderness of human need as Jesus did. We are to be the salt of the earth, giving ourselves even to death to release life to those who do not know our Lord. **It is in the wilderness that we meet the Lord to experience his presence and see his glory and it is in the wilderness that we find the true opportunities to express his love for the world through the ministry in the power of the Spirit.** The problem we have is that many never move beyond the gates of religious control and those who do often turn back or if they do not turn back, they stop too soon. Our institutional mindsets cause those who do venture out to behave like Peter on the Mount of Transfiguration (Luke 9:28-36) – immediately when we experience an unusual manifestation of God's glory, we want to build something where we can camp. Somehow, we keep missing the point that God does not live inside buildings built by human hands! The Spirit cannot be enclosed in our walls!

I am writing this at a time that we are close to the end of a wilderness journey and an experience that literally cost us everything we had. In truth, the choices we made in obedience to the Spirit led us to a place where we lost most of what we had worked for most of our lives. In addition, we were stripped of much of our dignity and pride. Much of what we did and said made (and still makes) no sense to most people, including many friends and "church people." So, after an incredible battle as we began to see the first light at the end of the tunnel, it really struck me! Seeking some Biblical picture that would relate to where we were in the journey, I thought about the people of God finally getting close to crossing the river Jordan to enter the Promised Land. **It was then that I realized that ours is a continuing journey into the wilderness! We are called to the wilderness, for here we do not have an enduring city! Suddenly God opened my eyes to see the wilderness of this world in a way I had never seen it before. Through the release of the Spirit in and through us, the wilderness becomes changed and the glory of God is revealed as we minister to the needs of those with whom God sets up divine appointments for us and in whom we meet our Lord.**

Isaiah 41:17-20 reads as follows: *The poor and needy search for water, but there is none; their tongues are parched with thirst. But I the Lord will answer them; I, the God of Israel will not forsake them. I will make rivers flow on barren heights and springs within the valleys. I will turn the desert into pools of water and the parched ground into springs. I will put in the desert the cedar and the acacia, the myrtle and the olive. I will set pines in the wasteland, the fir and the cypress together, so that the people may see and know, may consider and understand, that the hand of the Lord had done this, that the Holy One of Israel has created it.* The same message is found in Isaiah 35 and also in Isaiah 43:14-21 where we among others find the words

"Forget the former things; do not dwell on the past. See I am doing a new thing! Now it springs up; do you not perceive it? I am making a way in the desert and streams in the wasteland."

These words were originally spoken in reference to the return of the exiles from the Babylonian captivity and picked up images from the exodus out of Egypt and the journey through the desert and the wilderness to the Promised Land. These events and words are prophetic pictures for the western church, which has been in a self-imposed Babylonian captivity, through the rejection of the order of Melchizedek and of the freedom of the Spirit, to follow the Levitical institutional model. In a very real way, the majority of those who consider themselves as Christians in the western world have returned to Egypt and rejected the freedom offered in Christ. The liberal theologians and church leaders, like the Pharaohs of old, use the labor and resources of many who do not know that they were called to freedom, to maintain their positions of power and to build their local empires. Many of the church buildings, like the pyramids of old, are monuments to the dead and to dead traditions for they bring no life to the world. They are based on empty ideas borrowed from worldly wisdom and rational thought clothed in religious jargon. Many of those known as evangelical Christians are like the Israelites who crossed through the Red Sea, but stopped right there. They keep looking back longing for the food of Egypt and are not willing to journey beyond their religious tradition. They have their "fire insurance policy," and little else matters. The closeness to Egypt means that many operate on the worldly system they had adopted in Egypt and they will not move into the wilderness to the mountain of the Lord and taste the power of the Spirit. The Charismatics are those who have seen and possibly experienced the power of the Spirit, but like the Israelites of old they have chosen to have a leader like Moses, who would represent them and meet with the Lord on their behalf and minister to them. They love the touch of an 'anointed man or woman of God,' but do not want to move further into the wilderness. In the words of Hebrews 13:13, they want to stay in the camp, refusing to go to the crucified Lord outside the camp and to bear the disgrace he bore. **However, as we read in Isaiah 43, the Lord is doing a new thing! He is calling his people out of Egypt and out of the Babylonian exile, into the wilderness.**

Looking back, I see that my journey was through the stages represented above. Step by step I walked away from all these things that hindered and let go of the religious baggage and as I did, I found that I was moving into the wilderness. I thought it would be just a journey through the wilderness to a Promised Land here, but as I said before, it dawned upon me that we are actually called into this wilderness to meet our God and be transformed to be his people expressing his love to the world. This truth can also be seen in the main feasts celebrated in Israel. The first is the Passover celebrating the freedom from slavery in Egypt. Jesus Christ became our Passover Lamb, setting us free from the slavery to sin. The second stage brought God's people to Sinai where they received the law and saw the manifestation of God's power. It was also the celebration of the first fruits of the harvest, called Pentecost. In the New Testament this coincided with the outpouring of the Spirit and the birth of the church. On that day the first fruits of the New Covenant in Christ were brought in and God's people were empowered by the Spirit to move into the world, from Jerusalem through Judea and Samaria to the ends of the earth. No longer did they need religious laws and regulations or Levitical priests to teach these, for the Spirit would guide all members of the Lord's body and put the law in their minds and write it on their hearts. The final feast is the feast of Tabernacles. This feast was a reminder of the wandering in the wilderness and the celebration of the great and final harvest. **This feast was celebrated by moving out of the comfort zones of the homes to live as small family groups in temporary shelters for seven days. Today the fields are ripe and, drawn by the love of God for the world, we are being sent by the Spirit into the fields to gather the harvest.**

The only account recorded of Jesus attending the feast of Tabernacles in Jerusalem is very revealing. We find this in John 7 and at the end we read the following in verses 37-39: *On the last and greatest day of the feast, Jesus stood up and said: "If anyone is thirsty, let him come to me and drink. Whoever believes in me, as the Scripture has said, streams of living water will flow from within him." By this he meant the Spirit, whom those who believe in him were later to receive. Up to that time the Spirit had not yet been given, since Jesus had not yet been glorified.* Before we look at these words in more depth, let us turn to the story in John 4 where Jesus met a lonely, rejected and broken woman at a well in Samaria. In the midst of the conversation with her in verses 13-14, referring to the water in the well, Jesus said: *"Everyone who drinks from this water will be thirsty again, but whoever drinks from the water I give him will never thirst. Indeed, the water I give him will become in him a spring of water, welling up to eternal life."* As the story unfolds this lady's life is completely turned around and she returns to the village and tells everyone that they need to meet the man that offered her the water of life. As they make their way to Jesus and his disciples, the latter were surprised that Jesus was no longer hungry. Seeing the people from the village coming with their needs, we read in John 4:34-35: *"My food," Jesus said, "is to do the will of him who sent me and to finish his work. Do you not say, 'Four months more and then the harvest'? I tell you, open your eyes and look at the fields! They are ripe for harvest."*

In the wilderness of our society there is a harvest of unprecedented proportions. There are needs that only our Lord can touch through the power of his Spirit. As it happened with the lady at the well, one changed life can become the catalyst to reach a town. However, this will only happen if we move out of our comfort zones and return to our first love. As western church we are best compared to the church in Laodicea, of which we read in Revelation 3:15-17: *I* *know your deeds, that you are neither cold nor hot. I wish you were either one or the other! So, because you are lukewarm – neither hot nor cold – I am about to spit you out of my mouth. You say, "I am rich; I have acquired wealth and do not need a thing." But you do not realize that you are wretched, pitiful, poor and blind.* Sunday by Sunday we meet in our buildings with pews and chairs, choirs, robes, stained glass windows and run the programs, while the world in need is forgotten and untouched. In the words of Isaiah 41:17: *The poor and needy search for water, but there is none; their tongues are parched with thirst.* We who have the water of life have bottled this up and locked it in our buildings and organizations in such ways that even those who come seldom taste the water of life. Like some of the exiles, we have become so satisfied in our self-imposed Babylonian exile that we do not want to give it up and return to rebuild the broken foundations and become the church we were called and destined to be.

In his grace our Lord is calling us as he did with the rich and satisfied exiles in Isaiah 55:1-6 and 8-13: *Come, all you who are thirsty, come to the waters; and you, who have no money, come, buy and eat! Come, buy wine and milk without money and without cost. Why spend your money on what is not bread, and your labor on what does not satisfy? Listen, listen to me, and eat what is good, and your soul will delight in the richest of fare. Give ear and come to me; hear me, that your soul may live. I will make an everlasting covenant with you, my faithful love promised to David. See, I have made him a witness to the peoples, a leader and commander of the peoples. Surely, you will summon nations you know not and nations that do not know you will hasten to you, because of the Lord your God, the Holy One of Israel, for he has endowed you with splendor. Seek the Lord while he may be found; call on him while he is near. "For my thoughts are not your thoughts, neither are your ways my ways," declares the Lord. "As the heavens are higher than the earth, so are my ways higher than your ways and my thoughts than your thoughts.* As I look back on our journey of faith, we have spent so much time, effort and resources on that which really did not satisfy. Our labor yielded little for the Kingdom. In the eyes of the world and of the world of the church, we were successful, yet in real terms, little of lasting value was achieved. We were so focused on building 'the church' in the ways of the world that we missed seeing the ripe fields. When we did get a little view of the potential harvest, we tried to gather what we could in our local barn and spent our resources on building bigger and better. In this we mostly missed the heartbeat of the Lord for the world and as long as we continue with the Levitical system, we will repeat this over and over. **It is time to face the truth and walk through the gates into the wilderness to be the church.**

Before we bring these thoughts together, we need to look at another picture from the Old Testament that relates to our Lord's call to us. The love of God for his people is the theme of the life and words of Hosea. The prophet in obedience to the Lord married an unfaithful woman and his married life was a prophetic picture of the relationship between God and his unfaithful people. In this marriage Hosea's love for Gomer became a picture of God's incredible love for his people and in Hosea

2:14-16 we read: *"Therefore I am now going to allure her; I will lead her into the desert and speak tenderly to her. There I will give her back her vineyards, and I will make the valley of Achor a door of hope. There will she sing as in the days of her youth, as in the day she came up from Egypt. In that day," declares the Lord, "you will call me 'my husband'; you will no longer call me 'my master.'"* **Today God is calling his church that has moved away from the foundations back to its roots. He is calling us into the wilderness to tabernacle (camp and spend time) with him. He is calling us to our first love and to personally know him again and become like the early church, the days of our youth. He is not interested in being served with buildings and religious programs, but that we would know him intimately and that we experience his love and share it with others.** As we personally got away from the busyness of religious church programs, we got time to spend with the Lord, so that we came to know him as 'husband' and not as 'master'. In the process we began to see through our Father's eyes the need in the world and experience his love for the world. As I said before, the Scriptures came alive in ways we had never known and much of our worldly wisdom covered up in religious clothing became revealed for what it really was. The pat religious answers did not cut it anymore and we faced overwhelming circumstances that forced us to trust God, as we never did before, for no one can survive the desert without the grace of God. In real terms we lost our vineyards, for as we walked out of the world of the church, we walked away from most of the ministry opportunities and connections we had been involved in for years. With that most of our income was cut and we began a journey that would cost us dearly to the point that our reputation and much more were lost. Like Israel we entered the valley of Achor where we experienced the judgment and discipline of God as he took us through the furnace of affliction and refined us for his own sake as he said in Isaiah 48:10-11.

In this wilderness the words of Psalm 42, especially verses 1-8, spoke to us as never before, for all we could do was cry out to the Lord:

As the deer pants for streams of water,
so my soul pants for you, o God.
My soul thirsts for God, for the living God.
When can I go and meet with God?
My tears have been my food day and night,
while men say to me all day long, "Where is your God?"
These things I remember as I pour out my soul:
how I used to go with the multitude, leading the procession to the house of God,
with shouts of joy and thanksgiving among the festive throng.
Why are you downcast, O my soul?
Why so disturbed within me?
Put your hope in God,
for I will yet praise him, my Savior and my God.
My soul is downcast within me;
therefore, I will remember you,
from the land of the Jordan,
from the heights of Hermon – from Mount Mizar.

Deep calls to deep, in the roar of your waterfalls;
all your waves and breakers have swept over me.
By day the Lord directs his love,
at night his song is with me – a prayer to the God of my life!

The journey into the wilderness was literally one that moved us away from most of what was our security and stability. Friends and family began to avoid us and question us. The worst part was we had no clear answers (and still don't have these), except our faith that, even though it made no sense, God was in it and we were to obey. In the midst of this we learned to live by faith and the promises of God became real in amazing ways. The big dreams seemed to be gone as we lost our vineyards. In time even the memories of 'the good old days' when I used to lead the processions faded. **Yet, in the deep God became real as our spirits connected with the Spirit of God** and he refreshed us through his love and a new song was put into our hearts. Instead of being involved in ministry with the big groups, God brought a few broken individuals on similar journeys to meet with us, and with them we came to experience what it means to be the church instead of doing the church programs. God set up the divine appointments and we came to meet him in the lives of people as he said in Matthew 25:31-45. We met some hurting and ministered to their needs and witnessed the power of ordinary people anointed to be extraordinary royal priests in the order of Melchizedek. In this process the water of life flowed from the innermost parts of ordinary believers into parched land to water the desert and it began to bloom as lives were touched and changed. **However, some divine appointments came with a price! The key divine appointment God set up for me was to walk with a few individuals following a dream that seemed to be moving further away than ever and which for the most part included walking in faith with one broken and hurting individual on an incredible journey. This journey of over 10 years took us on strange and unknown paths, through disappointments and to repeatedly face what seemed to be insurmountable obstacles. The choices we made in obedience to the Lord to help this one man would eventually cost us our home and the last little earthly security we had. Like Isaac in Genesis 26 we stayed in the land in obedience to God's word and sowed in the famine in ways we had never expected to do. According to the Scriptures Isaac reaped a hundred-fold the first year, but our famine deepened for years, until we sowed not only our seed, but our bread as well.** This part of our journey made the words of Isaiah 58:1-12 come alive as our old religious ways gave way to a new reality:

"Shout it aloud, do not hold back.
Raise your voice like a trumpet.
Declare to my people their rebellion
and to the house of Jacob their sins.
For day after day they seek me out;
they seem eager to know my ways,

as if they were a nation that does what is right
and has not forsaken the commands of its God.
They ask me for just decisions
and seem eager for God to come near them.
'Why have we fasted,' they say,
'and you have not seen it?
Why have we humbled ourselves,
and you have not noticed?'
Yet on the day of your fasting, you do as you please
and exploit all your workers!
Your fasting ends in quarreling and strife,
and in striking each other with wicked fists.
You cannot fast as you do today
and expect your voice to be heard on high.
Is this not the kind of fast I have chosen,
only a day for a man to humble himself?
Is it only for bowing a man's head like a reed
and for lying on sackcloth and ashes?
Is that what you call a fast,
a day acceptable to the Lord?
Is not this the kind of fasting I have chosen:
to loose the chains of injustice
and untie the cords of the yoke,
to set the oppressed free and break every yoke?
Is it not to share your food with the hungry,
and to provide the poor wanderer with shelter -
when you see the naked, to clothe him,
and not to turn away from your own flesh and blood?
Then your light will break forth like the dawn,
and your healing will quickly appear;
then your righteousness will go before you,

and the glory of the Lord will be your rear guard.
Then you will call and the Lord will answer;
you will cry for help, and he will say, 'Here am I!'
If you do away with the yoke of oppression,
with the pointing finger and malicious talk,
and if you spend yourselves in behalf of the hungry
and satisfy the needs of the oppressed,
then your light will rise in the darkness,
and your night will become like the noonday.
The Lord will guide you always;
he will satisfy your needs in a sun-scorched land
and will strengthen your frame.
You will be like a well-watered garden,
like a spring whose waters never fail.
Your people will rebuild the ancient ruins
and will raise up the age-old foundations;
you will be called Repairer of Broken Walls,
Restorer of Streets and Dwellings."

So, we walked into the wilderness and followed the Spirit as he directed us and set up divine appointments. As this happened, we faced overwhelming situations, yet we learned that it was indeed not through power or might, but through the Spirit. We literally spent ourselves in behalf of the hungry and poured what we had into the oppressed, even to the point of being shunned and rejected by close friends and relatives who did not understand. When we had no bread to give, we unashamedly knocked on doors to ask for bread for our friend (Luke 11:5-10) and we watched how God provided at times in ways we could never imagine!

The Spirit released a well flowing from deep within us and even though we walked in the wilderness with nothing, often thirsty ourselves, we were able to be a well-watered garden for our friend and for others and we saw the spring never failing to bring forth water out of the desperately dry ground. We saw the same happen with others around us and as we continued to give, like the widow who kept pouring into the empty vessels, the flow was there when needed. **The desert literally bloomed as the thirsty received water and the most unlikely vessels blossomed in the wilderness. Instead of building "our church and ministry", we simply released life and healing and worked to restore the age-old foundations and rebuild the ancient ruins. We saw the Lord take over to build his church, without programs and clergy and physical buildings, as lives including our own were changed. All we needed to do was to walk in obedience and be available to do the work of ministry and to release others as we moved on, even if they did not have it all together as we might think they should have.**

In a literal way we have come to the end of this phase of our journey into the wilderness. In many ways at this point we have not seen the final completion for which we worked – much like the heroes of faith recalled in Hebrews 11 of whom we read at the end of that chapter that they "*were commended for their faith, yet none of them received what had been promised. God had planned something better for us, so that only together with us would they be made perfect.*" So in the midst of a strange journey having worked to help a man who, in many ways did not and do not seem to appreciate the sacrifice of many, God worked in our lives through the process to open our eyes to see in ways we never did and to change us and teach us to trust him above all. At the same time this book has reached its completion and for those who stayed with us to read to this point, there is a challenge and a promise. The challenge is to step out of the world of the church and enter the wilderness in obedience to the Spirit to release the living water so that the desert may bloom and flourish. The promise is from Amos 9:11-15 that reads as follows:

"In that day I will restore David's fallen tent.
I will repair its broken places,
restore its ruins and build it as it used to be,
so that they may possess the remnant of mankind
and all nations that bear my name,"
declares the Lord, who will do these things.
"The days are coming," declares the Lord,
"when the reaper will be overtaken by the plowman
and the planter by the one treading grapes.
New wine will drip from the mountains and flow from all the hills.
I will bring back my exiled people Israel;
they will rebuild the ruined cities and live in them.
They will plant vineyards and drink their wine;
they will make gardens and eat their fruit.
I will plant Israel in their own land,

never again to be uprooted from the land I have given them," says the Lord your God.

There is a promise of an unprecedented harvest and restoration of true Kingdom proportions. Prophetically many in the church have sensed that these words are for this day and age. However, true to the Institutional Church paradigm, they have interpreted these words to mean the establishment of great worship centers like the tabernacle of David that was set up in Jerusalem and preceded the building of the temple by Solomon. The history and background to this tent where the Ark of the Covenant was placed is fascinating, but it will take us too far from our focus.[13] In short, the ark was taken from the tent of meeting in Shiloh during a battle against the Philistines who won the battle and captured the ark. At the time the daughter-in-law of the priest Eli gave birth to a boy and called him Ichabod as the glory of God had departed with the ark from Israel. The tent of meeting and the rest of the furnishings were moved to Gibeon, where the rituals and offerings continued with the Holy of Holies darkened as the ark and the presence of God was not there anymore. When the ark was returned to Israel it was not brought back into its place in the tent of meeting. It was moved to different places until David brought it back to Jerusalem where he set up the tent to house it. Thus, throughout the reign of the

---

[13] I do recommend the chapter entitled "five mountains" in the book "The eternal purpose" by George Davis and Michael Clark (see the website http://awildernessvoice.com) for details.

fleshly-minded Saul the rituals and worship continued at Gibeon, even though the glory of the Lord and his presence in the Most Holy place was not there! Further, when David finally brought the ark to Jerusalem and set it up in the tent, it was no longer hidden from sight of all except the High Priest. It was visible to all and a new priesthood under Zadok ministered to the Lord at the tent. **This was a prophetic picture of what was to come. The need for an earthly priest (or pastor!) to minister as mediator between God and his people would be no more. God's glory would be visible to ordinary people as the High Priest in the order of Melchizedek (The king of righteousness – Zedek from where the name Zadok comes) opened the door to the inner sanctuary and brought the glory of God to be visible to ordinary people able to enter into the presence of God in his name.**

It is vitally important to recognize that the old Levitical ministry continued in Gibeon without the presence of God for generations, even while the tent of David brought the glory of God to ordinary people in Jerusalem. Many years after that Jesus, the Son of David died outside the walls of Jerusalem and the curtain in the temple was torn as sign that the presence and glory of God had again moved from the earthly temple to be seen and experienced by ordinary people in the order of Melchizedek. In the words of Jesus to the Samaritan woman in John 4:21-24: *"Believe me, woman, a time is coming when you will worship the Father neither on this mountain nor in Jerusalem. You Samaritans worship what you do not know; we worship what we do know, for salvation is from the Jews. Yet a time is coming and has now come when the true worshipers will worship the Father in spirit and in truth, for they are the kind of worshipers the Father seeks. God is Spirit and his worshipers must worship in spirit and in truth."* Yet, even as the early believers moved away from the temple and from Jerusalem and the order of Melchizedek opened homes and streets to be places of true worship, with the Spirit's power confirming the ministry through healing and salvations, the old Levitical order continued to repeat the empty rituals in the temple just like their ancestors did at Gibeon! **This is again prophetic for the institutional church which chose to follow the Levitical order and today many are caught in the empty religious practices in earthly temples with priests and programs, while the glory of God's presence has moved away. This glory is now released in the most unlikely places, most often in ordinary homes where two or three meet in the name of Jesus.**

It is further very important to note that the promise of the restoration of David's fallen tent in Amos 9 was picked up in the New Testament in the context of the debate on circumcision in the church. In short, there were those who wanted to have the laws and practices of the Levitical covenant forced upon the Gentile believers. The experiences of Peter when he shared the gospel with the Gentiles in Cornelius' house and those of Barnabas and Paul on their mission journeys and particularly the fact that God poured out the Spirit on the new believers without them having been circumcised proved decisive. James in quoting the words of Amos suggested that there be no Levitical requirements placed upon the Gentile believers and the church accepted that. As the tent of David opened the way for ordinary people to experience the glory and presence of God, so would it be in the church wherever God's people meet in the name of Jesus. The harvest would be brought in without the need for religious practices, rituals, clergy or buildings! All that was needed would be to minister in the name of Jesus and in the power of the Spirit.

This was already revealed in the words of Amos in a powerful way. **Anyone who can read Hebrew will recognize that the word used for 'tent' in this context is not the same word used to describe the tabernacle of David in Jerusalem. This is not accidental. Amos chose the word that described the temporary shelters erected during the Feast of Tabernacles. This word is also the tie to the gathering of the harvest as recognized by the early church as they dealt with the question whether Gentiles brought into the church needed to be circumcised, for those bringing in the harvest lived in such temporary shelters in the fields.** Using this term for the fallen tent of David also brings to mind the time he spent in the wilderness living in temporary shelters and being persecuted by Saul. It was precisely during this time that God prepared David for his call and brought around him those who were to become his key support and future leaders, as we read in 1 Samuel 22:1-2: *David left Gath and escaped to the cave of Adullam. When his brothers and his father's household heard about it, they went down to him there. All those who were in distress or in debt or discontented gathered around him and he became their leader. About four hundred men were with him.* This is prophetic for the church as we enter into the first phase of the great harvest. God is calling forth servant leaders who will among others attract the least likely people as they move into the wilderness, just like David did. We are called to release the water of life and minister healing to the wounded and hurting. These unlikely ones will in time become the core of harvesters. They will be the most effective workers, for they will be able to relate to those in the wilderness and in turn release healing and restoration to the needy until the desert becomes fruitful. The fields are ready for the harvest and as we venture out into the world in obedience to the call of God, we pray and God sets up divine appointments – often with the least likely individuals. As we practice true fasting and spend ourselves in their behalf, they receive the touch of the Lord on their lives and are being equipped by the Spirit to bear fruit and gather the harvest. Our prayers to the Father for workers to gather the harvest are answered in these divine appointments in the wilderness and they set in motion a continuous process of sowing and reaping.

The prophetic word in Amos is thus not about worship in the traditional sense of the word. It is about worship defined in Romans 12:1. It flows from the heart where God's people *in view of his mercy offer their bodies as living sacrifices, holy and acceptable to God in a spiritual act of worship, breaking the pattern of the world manifested in the world of the church paradigm, being transformed by the renewing of their minds.* Stepping out of the world of the church in obedience to the Spirit to be royal priests totally submitted to the Lord, the wilderness is transformed and the captives are set free, equipped and released to do the work of ministry. Ordinary homes become places where the glory of God is revealed through the power of his Spirit, as ordinary people minister in simple childlike faith to the needs of the world that they encounter.

The same is true for gatherings of God's people to worship in spirit and in truth. As we walked into the wilderness and God connected us with others who have done the same, we tried to bring various house churches together for times of celebration. At first our intent was to set up a network of house churches as we shared earlier, but then we realized that it is simply the old roots of the Institutional Church paradigm sprouting new growth. Yet, we did feel the need for occasional larger gatherings where we could encourage one another and celebrate in ways that would allow different expressions of worship. It was easy to rent the facilities of a local church on a Saturday evening and have all the equipment needed available and cover cost with a simple freewill offering. However, after a while we stopped – knowing there was something in this, but also something more was needed. Looking back, I now see that the first celebrations we organized partly flowed from the institutional baggage we had not shed, particularly the baggage of "corporate worship" discussed earlier. However, there was much more to this. As we prayed and pondered the matter, God spoke a major word of revelation to me through one of the friends that has walked much of the early journey with us. Even though it is not necessarily wrong to rent an existing church building for an occasional celebration and to sing and celebrate God's grace with a crowd, the whole idea is that we are to move into the world even with our celebrations! It is like the story of Zacchaeus: observing the scene of the crowd from a tree branch, his life is turned around and it ends in a celebration at his home. A prodigal son returns and the Father rejoices and the fattened calf is killed for a huge party. Parties like these allow us to join with many who need to connect with the life offered in Christ. In our celebration and joy, they witness the light they need and experience true worship. In the words of the Messianic prophecy in Isaiah 9:1-2:

The people that walk in darkness have seen a great light;
on those living in the land of the shadow of death a light has dawned.
You have enlarged the nation and increased their joy;
they rejoice before you as people rejoice at the harvest,
as men rejoice when dividing the plunder.

We are called out of our self-imposed exile and away from the confining Levitical structures into the world so that the wilderness is changed. The light within us cannot be hidden and should not be hidden in buildings and under steeples. It has to be taken to the highways and byways of our communities and the darkness driven away. The thirsty have to receive the waters of life released from our innermost beings and the harvest has to be brought in so that the joy of the Lord burst forth and release spontaneous celebrations in our streets and work places as the captives are released and the sick healed.

As we get ready for the harvest and the return of our Lord, there is a wonderful story that he told us in Matthew 22:2-14: *The kingdom of heaven is like a king who prepared a wedding banquet for his son. He sent his servants to those who had been invited to the banquet to tell them to come, but they refused to come. He sent more servants and said: "Tell those that had been invited that I have prepared my dinner: my oxen and fattened cattle have been butchered and everything else is ready. Come to the wedding banquet."*

But they paid no attention and went off – one to his field, another to his business. The rest seized his servants, mistreated them and killed them. The king was enraged. He sent his army and destroyed those murderers and burned their city.

Then he said to his servants: "The wedding banquet is ready, but those I invited did not deserve to come. Go to the street corners and invite to the banquet anyone you find." So the servants went out into the streets and gathered all the people they could find, both good and bad, and the wedding hall was filled. But when the king came in to see the guests, he noticed a man there who was not wearing wedding clothes. "Friend," he asked, "how did you get in here without wedding clothes?" The man was speechless. Then the king told the attendants: "Tie him hand and foot and throw him outside into the darkness, where there will be weeping and gnashing of the teeth. For many are invited, but few are chosen."

This story speaks for itself. Our Lord came to this world as he himself said to seek and save the lost. As his followers we are called into the wilderness and sent to the highways and byways of our communities to invite all we can find to the wedding feast. There is a choice to be made and the time is now. In the words of Paul in 2 Corinthians 6:1-2: *As God's fellow workers we urge you not to receive God's grace in vain. For he says: "In the time of my favor I heard you, and in the day of salvation I helped you." I tell you, now is the time of God's favor, now is the day of salvation.* God's grace was poured into us when Jesus Christ suffered and died outside the walls of Jerusalem. It was entrusted to us to share with the world in need. For too long we have kept it for ourselves inside the walls of religious traditions that we built in his name. It is time to lay our ambitions, our traditions and our religious kingdoms on the altar and follow the waters of life into the wilderness so that life may come forth. Let us hear the prophetic words of Ezekiel 47:1-12:

The man brought me back to the entrance of the temple, and I saw water coming from under the threshold of the temple toward the east (for the temple faced east). The water was coming from under the south side of the temple, south of the altar. Then he brought me out through the north gate and led me around the outside of the outer gate facing east, and the water was flowing from the south side.

As the man went eastward with a measuring line in his hand, he measured off a thousand cubits and then led me through water that was ankle-deep. He measured off another thousand cubits and led me through water that was knee-deep. He measured off another thousand, but now it was a river that I could not cross, because the water had risen and was deep enough to swim in – a river that no one could cross. He asked me: "Son of man, do you see this?"

Then he led me back to the bank of the river. When I arrived there, I saw a great number of trees on each side of the river. He said to me, "This water flows toward the eastern region and goes down into the Arabah, where it enters the Sea. When it empties the Sea the water there becomes fresh. Swarms of living creatures will live wherever the river flows. There will be large numbers of fish, because the water flows there and makes the salt water fresh; so where the river flows, everything will live. Fishermen will stand along the shore; from En Gedi to En Eglaim there will be places for spreading nets. The fish will be of many kinds – like the fish of the Great Sea. But the swamps and the marshes will not become fresh; they will be left for salt. Fruit trees of all kinds will grow on both banks of the river. Their leaves will not wither, nor will their fruit fail. Every month they will bear, because the water from the sanctuary flows to them. Their fruit will serve for fruit and their leaves for healing."

When the Lamb of God died on the cross, the veil in the temple was torn from top to bottom. With that the Levitical order with its priesthood, temple and religious programs was abolished and the High Priest in the order of Melchizedek entered the Most Holy Place once and for all. He opened the way for every one of us to boldly enter into the presence of the Father as royal priests. Living water began to flow from the altar out into the world. On the day of Pentecost, the Spirit was poured out and the living water was released from the innermost being of every believer that is born of water and the Spirit. It begins as a trickle when we lay our lives on the altar and as we walk through the gates of religious control and follow our Lord, bearing the disgrace he bore, the flow increases. The further we move into the wilderness of this world and minister in his name, the more the flow of life-giving water which transforms even the most barren region, yes even the Dead Sea, to bring forth life, with food, fruit and healing. This is why Paul wrote in 2 Corinthians 6:1-2, *As God's fellow workers we urge you not to receive God's grace in vain. For he says: "In the time of my favor I heard you, and in the day of salvation I helped you." I tell you, now is the time of God's favor, now is the day of salvation.* It is indeed the time of salvation and favor of our Lord and you and I have been equipped to release the water of life so that the desert may bloom and flourish. **I urge you to step into your call as a royal priest in the power and anointing of the Spirit. Make your life count for the sake of the Kingdom. May those who have ears hear the Spirit!**

APPENDIX

Through this book we have made reference to a number of resources that I have written as we embarked on this journey of faith. We recommend that you read the following if you have not done so before:

Restoring the broken foundations

This book is the first in the series and addresses the foundational issues about the church and why the new wine will tear the old structures. It covers topics like the history of the church structures, fivefold ministry, the untapped resource of members' gifts, the models of Biblical leadership and sacred cows of Charismatic Christianity and the foundations of Covenant relationships.

Ordinary people extraordinary royal priests

This book followed as God led me on a journey through the letter to the Hebrews and the fact that in Christ the Levitical priesthood was replaced with the order of Melchizedek. Recognizing that the Western Church's structure is a semi-Christianized version of the Levitical model that replaced the New Testament model since the early century, it cannot simply be changed to accommodate the new wine. We need a total new wineskin to allow the priesthood of the believer to function. This is a foundational book on the priesthood of the believer and a call to walk out of the comfort zones of unfruitful faith.

Radical Authenticity

This Book followed the first two in taking this vision to the practical realities of how to be the church and walk in The Way. It is a call to walk in The Way and to be the church – a call to be radically authentic.

Arise and Shine Ekklesia – Make your home a place where people meet Jesus

This book is a practical guide to having and hosting house churches. It gives direction on how to make your home a place where people can meet Jesus, based on his promise to show up where two or three are gathered in his name. It is a vital resource for anyone interested to start a house church.

I ask and encourage readers to do reviews of the books and publish them. As author I would truly appreciate that and they do make a difference. Thanks.

Willie Joubert

ABOUT THE AUTHOR

Dr. Willie Joubert was born in what was known as Tanganyika in East Africa and grew up on a farm that his parents pioneered after World War 2. It was an amazing childhood growing up in amidst wild animals with no hydro, phones, radios or TVs! When he was 11 they moved to a farm in South Africa. Going to school in the nearby town unbeknownst to him at the time was the fact that one of his classmates in Grade 6 would be his future wife. For those interested, Willie has also written a book covering the lives of his parents and it is available as eBook on Amazon – A Century on African Soil.

Following graduation, he attended the University of Pretoria where he completed a Master's degree in Semitic Languages and a degree in Theology and subsequently a Ph.D. in Old Testament Studies. Dr. Joubert taught Semitic Languages for 7 years at the University of Pretoria before he immigrated to Canada with his wife, Eda, and three children. In Canada he pastored in traditional churches as Presbyterian Minister and then in non-denominational settings, worked in church planting as well as in prayer ministry and applying his faith in business settings and in support of para-church ministries. These journeys led to a re-examining of the Biblical foundations of the Church and a conclusion that the future of the church will necessitate a return to the simplicity of the early church in small home-based churches where ordinary people will do the work of ministry.

With this conviction Willie and Eda pioneered a home church and began to network with others. In the process he wrote a number of books and shared the copies with friends and with anyone interested in these. Recently he decided to formally publish these books so that a wider audience can tap into the resources. This book is the last in the series 'Being the Church in the World.' As stated, it covers the key practical issues and the challenges that they faced as they moved out of their comfort zone of the Institutional Church to pursue the Way described in the Book of Acts and in the pages of the New Testament. May it be a help to those who dream that the Church can be more than what they have experienced so far!

CPSIA information can be obtained
at www.ICGtesting.com
Printed in the USA
LVHW080546031121
702323LV00008B/460